Craft Beer Design

The Design, Illustration, and Branding of
Contemporary Breweries

gestalten

LA *Sweep*

DES **CANTONS** DEPUIS 2016

RED IPA **BIO**

473 M

Table of Contents

Cheers!

Lift your glass, because this is a celebration: a toast to the craft brewers and especially the designers behind all the stellar craft beer brands of today's world. 49 breweries and designers are featured in this book showcasing the immensely talented artists working hard to make beautiful homes for the tasty beer inside. Without these artists we probably wouldn't drink as much, and I for one certainly wouldn't enjoy it in the same way. But when it comes to vices, I don't think obsessing over beer is the worst you can have. So let's delight in all these fantastic-looking breweries—and what better way to do that than to open a beer and dive right into their amazing designs.

PETER MONRAD

Peter Monrad is a Copenhagen-based graphic designer with years of experience in branding, art direction, design for mobile apps, and various international start-ups. He's also an avid consumer of IPA and a musician/producer releasing music under the moniker Tiny Anthem.

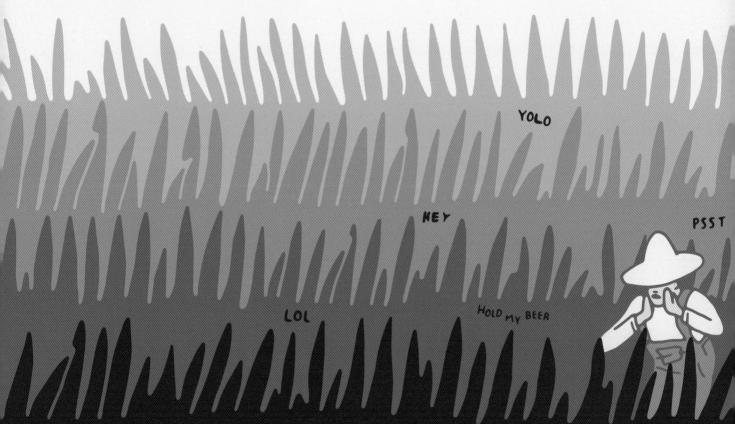

Basqueland

LOCATION
Gipuzkoa, Spain

DESIGN
Marcos Navarro

BASQUELAND

HOP TIGER

DDH IPA

INGREDIENTES: Agua, cebada, trigo, levadura, lúpulos, CO2. **Contiene gluten.**
INGREDIENTS: Water, barley, wheat, yeast, hops, CO2. **Contains gluten.**
INGREDIENTS: Eau, orge, blé, levure, houblon, CO2. **Contient du gluten.**
INGREDIENTI: Acqua, orzo, grano, lievito, luppolo, CO2. **Contiene glutine.**
ZUTATEN: Gerstenmalz, Weizen, Hefe, Hopfen, CO2. **Enthält Gluten.**
Brewed and Packaged / Elaborado y Empaquetado

BASQUELAND BREWING CO.S.L.S0#:
ADDRESS – Pol. Akarregi, parcela 49,
Nº Hernani, 20120 Gipuzkoa. CONSUMIR
PREFERENTEMENTE ANTES DE: ver base /
CONSOMMER DE PRÉFÉRENCE AVANT:
voir sous la bouteille/ MINDESTENS
HALTBAR BIS: siehe boden/
SEE BASE FOR BEST
BEFORE DATE.
Unpasteurized. Unfined. Unfiltered.

18

MARCOS
NAVARRO

BPA
FREE

Operating from the heart of the Basque Country, Basqueland is dedicated to crafting beer on par with the area's culinary expertise, while their kaleidoscopic designs are both evocative and provocative.

How would you describe the visual style of your brewery?

Kevin Patricio (Co-Founder): We try to match the creativity on the label with the creativity our brewers apply to the beer—and vice versa! Our designs are colorful and visually stimulating. We have design aesthetics that range from simple to complex, textural to sleek, and intricate to wild.

Marcos Navarro (Artist and Illustrator): Basqueland is characterized by bold images packed with color, sometimes showing extremely happy moments, other times dark symbolism.

What is the process for designing the label for a new release?

MN: Normally we start with the naming. Ben or Kevin, the brewery founders, send me the beer name or maybe they have an idea. From that point I think about the theme, and I really like to explore the boundaries of possibility, take the design to the edge. We believe it's important to maintain an experimental process and spontaneity.

Where does the inspiration for the labels come from?

MN: Often illustrators think by drawing and the idea comes up as the pencil flows. Depending on the topic, I read about certain things or visit my symbology bible, which is always useful—or I just go surfing and clear my mind.

Which of your labels are you most proud of?

MN: I have to say I'm quite happy with them all, because every beer deserves my work and effort, and these are all so different. I'm definitely proud of the ones with the same style I would use in one of my original paintings—more personal-looking artwork.

What role do your visual identity and beer labels play in the success of your brand?

KP: Our art definitely plays a role in our success. The visual identity of the brand creates an expectation. The can art is the first impression for so many people who have never seen or tasted a Basqueland beer. The expectation is that if we care that much about how our can looks, we must care as much or more about the liquid, which we do! We drink with our eyes first.

Can you name two breweries whose visual styles you admire?

MN: Mikkeller—I really like their bold characters, their use of color, and illustrated type. Also their artists sell signed prints and special merch from the brewery, which is cool. Omnipollo is experimental and weird. They do crazy merch, painted trucks, and their church brewery is insane. Congrats folks! ▲

Halo Brewery

LOCATION
Toronto, Canada

DESIGN
Underline Studio

Brewing out of Toronto's Junction Triangle, Halo makes ales rooted in the Belgian and American brewing philosophies of artistry and experimentation. Their joy in unconventional ingredients is reflected in their adventurous, abstract labels.

SAISON WITH ROSE HIPS

TEST PATTERN (COLUMBUS)

5.1%
ABV

500ml
VOL

500ml
VOL

IPA

DRY HOPPED GOSE

DOUBLE LUCKY

6.4%
ABV

500ml
VOL

NEW WAVE

6.7%
ABV

500ml
VOL

CROSSTALK

0%

500ml
VOL

FOREIGN EXTRA STOUT WITH SARSAPARILLA

SOUR IPA

EVENT HORIZON

6.0%
ABV

500ml
VOL

ABV

GOSE WITH STRAWBERRY AND KIWI

SHAPESHIFTER

6.5%
ABV

473ml
VOL

DRY HOPPED PALE ALE

Each label is intended to convey a very directed and purposeful meaning through simplicity and abstraction.

CALLUM HAY
Co-Founder and Head Brewer

How would you describe the visual style of your brewery?

Callum Hay (Co-Founder and Head Brewer): Clean, minimalist, high-contrast, and geometric—there is a primary focus on line and shape across all our labels. In terms of other art styles, there are definitely elements of Bauhaus, De Stijl, and Dada, with occasional nods to specific movements such as Memphis, art deco, and art nouveau. Each label is intended to convey a very directed and purposeful meaning through simplicity and abstraction.

What is the process for designing the label for a new release?

CH: The process always starts with an email to Underline; I'll write an overview of the beer (name, style, ABV, etc.) and a brief for it. I try to make the brief as comprehensive as possible and include the ideas and definitions I want incorporated into the design. I'll also do some basic brainstorming for potential design directions.

Underline Studio: Callum's briefs are awesome, they are a fantastic starting point for us. He is highly creative in his naming of the beers, the concepts behind them, and how they relate to the beers themselves. As designers who start by understanding content and concept, this is a really critical part of the process for us. We explore multiple directions that we then narrow down to three or four to present to Callum. There is quite a library of labels now, so we also look at the rest of the family and how each can be unique. Once a direction for the graphics is settled, we often explore multiple color combinations until we settle on one.

Where does the inspiration for the labels come from?

CH: From my perspective, the beer name drives the inspiration. They are a mix of cultural references that appeal to me combined with elements of personal experience and the style

and characteristics of the beer itself. When I put together a brief, I try to abstract the ideas behind the label (knowing that our label art is inherently abstract) and distill the concept(s) being conveyed so that there are some coherent, brainstormy jump-off points.

Which of your labels are you most proud of?

CH: My favorites are New Wave, Kaleidoscope, Impossible Geometries, and our collection of anniversary labels. I love the simplicity of these labels but also how clearly they illustrate their purpose—all our labels do this, but these ones appeal to some of my favorite art styles and/or stand out for their eye-catching elegance and poignance.

US: How can we pick one from all our children? Everyone in our studio would have their own favorite.

What role do your visual identity and beer labels play in the success of your brand?

US: From the beginning the goal was to set Halo apart from the sea of sameness when it comes to smaller craft breweries. There is a very common visual language in this category and we strove to differentiate Halo from the rest. It is an adventurous brewery as well, with lots of experimentation and we wanted to create a brand that matched its unconventional sensibilities.

Can you name two breweries whose visual styles you admire?

CH: The first brewery would be Homes—their wild geometric designs and the eclectic range of their labels (everything from inkblot-like patterns to stripy-stippled op-art-like, moiré-inducing stuff) is super fun and beautiful to look at. The second is Other Half Brewing—their labels are simple, bright, stark, and just generally fun to look at. They use pattern and color to amazing effect. It's a great style for labeling beer; it makes me want to reach for it. ▲

SHAPESHIFTER

6.5% | 473ml

NEW WAVE

IPA

6.7% | 500ml
ABV | VOL

EVENT HORIZON

FOREIGN EXTRA STOUT WITH SARSAPARILLA

6.0% | 500ml
ABV | VOL

MAGIC MISSILE

DRY HOPPED PALE ALE

5.5% | 500ml
ABV | VOL

Mikkeller

LOCATION
Copenhagen, Denmark

DESIGN
Keith Shore (Art Director),
Luke Cloran (Designer)

When we think of the European craft movement, we often think of Mikkeller. This game-changing Danish brewery has garnered a global fanbase, not just for its crisp pints, but its ultra-recognizable design aesthetic.

How would you describe the visual style of your brewery?

Keith Shore (Art Director): Our design and drawing style is loose and colorful. The labels are lighthearted and our characters are strange and lovable.

What is the process for designing the label for a new release?

KS: We are typically given a name from the brewers and they might also give us a little background on why they chose it. I'll talk over conceptual ideas with our designer and then we will make a very rough sketch. Once we're on the same page, we render a final sketch, go over some different colorways, and I'll nitpick some little details until it feels ready to submit to print.

Where does the inspiration for the labels come from?

KS: Each label shares a little story about our characters, Henry and Sally. Sometimes we use the beer style or ingredients as a starting point to guide the narrative.

Which of your labels are you most proud of?

KS: Burst and our series of Sparkling Alcoholic Waters.

Can you name two breweries whose visual styles you admire?

KS: Omnipollo and De Dolle Brouwers. ▲

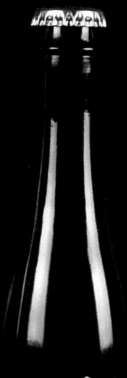

Stevns-bær

Bière des Champs

BLEND

I Would Not Feel So All Alone

Les Bières Horizon

LOCATION
Montreal, Canada

DESIGN
Tommy Øberg

Québecois brewers with a space-age, graphic identity, Les Bières Horizon creates adventurous beers for "dreamers and travelers" in their brewery north of Montreal.

How would you describe the visual style of your brewery?

Tommy Øberg (Designer): I wanted to create a brand that lingers between strict Swiss grid-style, and a somewhat playful take on geometric shapes, with a typographic grid as the backbone of the whole brand and on the cans.

What is the process for designing the label for a new release?

TØ: A constant inspirational flow and a tight ongoing conversation with the brewery end up in a mood board presentation of style, colors, name, etc. Then we decide which route to follow, finalize the artwork, and create social-media content, sell-sheets, and whatever necessary visuals are needed surrounding each drop.

Where does the inspiration for the labels come from?

TØ: Drinking beer, ha! There is a bit of seriousness in that for sure; I love experiencing beer brands, and drinking a good beer isn't a bad thing either. Other than that, I find much inspiration in Swiss design, minimalistic expressions, patterns, and op-art.

Which of your labels are you most proud of?

TØ: I was super-excited to start this project, and the first beer I did was Oberon. From the beginning it looked a bit different, but I really enjoyed finalizing and creating the graphic grid for the noise pattern and combining it with the Horizon typography. Helios is another personal favorite. I like the clean graphic, the clash between black and white, and the contrast between the thin lines and the heavy boxes.

What role do your visual identity and beer labels play in the success of your brand?

TØ: In short, the client brief was to engage beer geeks, gamers, and designers. Hopefully my work attracts them, and others. So far the response has been great.

Can you name two breweries whose visual styles you admire?

TØ: There are so many great brands and breweries out there. Top of mind—and completely different from what I've done with Horizon—but I love Karl Grandin's work for Omnipollo. For me, they are pioneers when it comes to creating beautiful label art. And I also enjoy a lot of the things To Øl creates. ▲

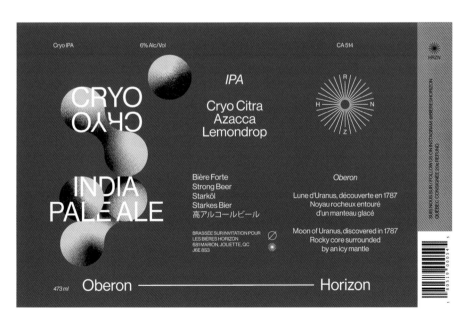

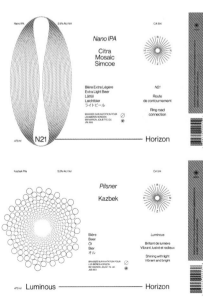

Bellwoods Brewery

LOCATION
Toronto, Canada

DESIGN
Doublenaut

With frameable labels and a loyal cult following, Toronto's Bellwoods Brewery produces an ever-evolving array of small-batch beers for the city's aficionados.

How would you describe the visual style of your brewery?

Bellwoods Brewery: The visual style of the brewery's artwork has evolved throughout the past decade in tandem with our beers. We were drawn to the bold colors, simplicity, and textural quality of Doublenaut's style early on, and have enjoyed the collaborative process of bringing beer concepts to life through label design.

What is the process for designing the label for a new release?

Doublenaut: Our process is pretty straight-forward: Bellwoods provides us with the name of the beer, a description, and the info that needs to appear on the label. Sometimes they have specific art direction, otherwise they'll leave it up to our interpretation. We'll do any necessary research about the hops, fruit, or other ingredients that go into the beer and then begin sketching out potential ideas. Once we have a strong concept, we provide Bellwoods with a refined sketch or mock-up for approval. Once a direction is approved, we execute the final design of the label and explore various color palettes that best suit the design.

Where does the inspiration for the labels come from?

D: Most of the visual direction for the labels comes from Bellwoods' creative names. However, some are less literal than others, which is what leads to our more abstract concepts.

Which of your labels are you most proud of?

D: We're most proud of some of the older, classic labels that have lived on and are still being used today: Wizard Wolf, Monogamy, Motley Cru, Jelly King, and Cat Lady. We're also fond of some of the newer, more abstract labels ▶

like Come What May and Goblin Sauce. We've enjoyed working on some collaborative beer labels over the past year that Bellwoods have been making with other breweries, like Goblin's Trill and BuWoo. It's also been fun to strip things down for the retro-inspired Pilsner series.

What role do your visual identity and beer labels play in the success of your brand?
BB: Our eclectic labels have been a draw for the brewery since the early days, and our general impression is that they might attract a wider audience than if we'd stuck to more conventional label design. They also just emphasize that we value creativity in all forms— whether it's beer recipes or beer packaging.

Can you name two breweries whose visual styles you admire?
BB: Revel Cider (not exactly beer, but a fellow Ontario alcohol producer) have crafted a really beautiful style. And we've always loved Willibald's branding. ▲

The Establishment Brewing Company

LOCATION
Calgary, Canada

DESIGN
Daughter Creative

The brainchild of a crew of music-loving friends, The Establishment Brewing Company makes world-class brews with sleek monochrome visuals that are a palette-cleansing tonic in the craft beer scene.

AUTOBAHN
MUNICH DUNKEL

BEER/BIÈRE
473ML 5.2% ALC./VOL.

SOCIAL CANDY
IMPERIAL NEW ENGLAND IPA

STRONG BEER/BIÈRE FORTE
473ML 8.5% ALC./VOL.

MY BEST FRIEND'S GIRL
KÖLSCH-STYLE ALE

BEER/BIÈRE
473ML 4.8% ALC./VOL.

ATARAXIA
IMPERIAL NEIPA

EXTRA STRONG BEER/BIÈRE EXTRA FORTE
473ML 8.0% ALC./VOL.

FLOAT ALONG
IMPERIAL NEW ENGLAND IPA

STRONG BEER/BIÈRE FORTE
473ML 8.2% ALC./VOL.

SUPER FUSION
CATHARINA SOUR WITH PINK GUAVA

BEER/BIÈRE
473ML 5.5% ALC./VOL.

GHOST MACHINE

DOUBLE DRY HOPPED IMPERIAL NEIPA
STRONG BEER/BIÈRE FORTE 473ML 8.5% ALC./VOL.

JAM ROCK
BLACKBERRY SOUR WITH VANILLA

STRONG BEER/BIÈRE FORTE
473ML 5.6% ALC./VOL.

CUT THE CAKE
IMPERIAL STOUT WITH CACAO NIBS

EXTRA STRONG BEER/BIÈRE EXTRA FORTE
473ML 10.5% ALC./VOL.

STRANGE POWERS
IMPERIAL NEW ENGLAND IPA

STRONG BEER/BIÈRE FORTE
473ML 8.4% ALC./VOL.

AFTERNOON DELIGHT
NEW ENGLAND PALE ALE

BEER/BIÈRE
473ML 5.4% ALC./VOL.

TWO TICKETS TO PARADISE
MANGO SOUR

BEER/BIÈRE
473ML 5% ALC./VOL.

In an incredibly cluttered retail market, choosing a black-and-white packaging system is bold, as is our rigid adherence to a gridded structure.

SIMON MACLEOD
Marketing Lead

How would you describe the visual style of your brewery?

Simon MacLeod (Marketing Lead): The brewery is built on a vision that pays reverence to old-school methods crafted in new-school ways. There is a strong connection between that philosophy and the Bauhaus style in terms of the transparency of process and ingredients, the rejection of unnecessary ornamentation for staunch simplicity, and the belief that science itself can be an art form. That all comes through in our geometric, gridded design system and in our color-palette.

What is the process for designing the label for a new release?

SM: It's centered around the beer name. Beer names are largely based on music we love, and that helps our design agency find inspiration for the labels—from the cellophane flowers in a Beatles song to the rhythmic waves of *Float Along.* Standard releases and core beers are white on black, and our Imperial New England IPA series is black on white with a new gloss-black on matte-black for our latest Imperial Stout line.

Where does the inspiration for the labels come from?

SM: The Establishment crew is connected by a love of music (and beer!) and those song titles and lyrics provide a warmth and quirk to a brand that is deliberately industrial in appearance. Visual inspiration for labels often stems from lyrics or album covers and is then transformed and executed within our gridded design system.

Which of your labels are you most proud of?

SM: Our Kölsch-style ale, My Best Friend's Girl, is a refreshingly simple combination of grainy pilsner malt, light apple and pear esters, and subdued hops. The label is a simplistic, stripped-down representation and nod to the classic Kölsch serving vessel—a *Stange* glass. Float Along was one of our first white-can

Imperial New England IPA releases, a series that pulls inspiration from psychedelic rock bands like King Gizzard & The Lizard Wizard. The rhythmic waves of the Float Along can really signify a perfect balance between soft bitterness and the kind of sweetness that only fruit at the brink of becoming over-ripe can bring. We love brewing classic beer styles as much as getting freaky and bending the rules. Jam Rock is a good example of pushing the boundaries of what beer can taste like. An irresponsible amount of blackberry was jammed into this kettle-soured beer, and that's evident with just one look.

What role do your visual identity and beer labels play in the success of your brand?

SM: In an incredibly cluttered retail market, choosing a black-and-white packaging system is bold, as is our rigid adherence to a gridded structure. The stark nature of our can labels is a fantastic contrast to the glorious hop juice inside and the shelf presence of a line-up of cores and seasonals is unmistakable. Having spent no money on traditional advertising, our organic growth has been driven by an interest in the packaging, and then an appreciation for the quality of the beer inside. People pick it up for the design, then buy it again for the amazing taste. Our highly distinctive visuals make it easy for them to find more of our brews to sample.

Can you name two breweries whose visual styles you admire?

SM: I like the simple, geometric, and confident style of Modern Times. Mikkeller is quirky but not overly complex or cluttered and with a strong artistic point of view. ▲

Merakai Brewing Co.

LOCATION
Sussex, U.K.

DESIGN
Motel Design

ILLUSTRATION
Laura Callaghan

Contains [allergens in bold]: Water, Hops, Yeast, Maltodextrine, **Gluten, Wheat, Barley, Oats.**
This Merakai Brewing Co. Beer was brewed and packaged at ABYSS Brewing LTD East Sussex, TN22 5RB, UK.

2.3 UK units. Please drink responsibly, for more info: merakaibrewing.com/drink-aware.

Vegan and vegetarian friendly. Aluminum recyclable. Never drink and drive.

IPA
Sour
Pilsner
Pale Ale
Lager

MERAKAI
BREWING
CO.

I'M YOU
BIGGEST F

5.2% ABV – DDH P

I'M YOUR BIGGEST FAN

Double dry hopped, tropical, and pillowy pale ale created for our supporters - old and new - who continue to inspire and lift us. Here's to you, cheers!

Hops: Mosaic, Ammarillo, Azacca ,Equanot

Store: Store Cold, Drink Fresh

Best Before: August 2021

Can: 440ml ℮

→ merakaibrewing.com
→ @merakai_brewing

Design:
motel.design
Illustration:
lauracallaghanillustration.com

5 060878 690005

Built on a foundation of inclusivity and openness, Merakai Brewing Co. puts their ethos on their cans with a diverse range of characters and points of view. They hope their welcoming business will create connections and start meaningful conversations.

How would you describe the visual style of your brewery?

Emma O'Neill-Parsons (Co-Founder): The visual style of the brewery represents who we are—it has a very distinctive point of view. I would describe it as challenging and inclusive. Challenging because the characters and visuals in the can artwork challenge who we think a craft beer drinker is, and inclusive because of the representation within the artwork. It's extremely important for us to use our packaging in this way. We wanted to create labels that spark a conversation, that make people want to pick us up and have a look to see what we're all about.

What is the process for designing the label for a new release?

EOP: Myself and Oliver Parsons (Co-Founder and Brewer) name our beers organically. I take the name as a starting point, create a backstory, and brief our illustrator Laura Callaghan on the direction. It takes approximately four weeks from start to finish. We have a label container designed by creative agency Motel Design, and each illustration is placed into the container and adjusted until we are happy with it.

Where does the inspiration for the labels come from?

Laura Callaghan (Illustrator): The brief for the illustrations was to design images that were packed with interest and detail, were colorful with a playful sense of fun. The beer names were a great jumping-off point and made my job a lot easier! I Licked It So It's Mine features characters feasting on ice cream at a carnival. We're Connected Aren't We? links characters through a series of connections, intertwined hair braids, tangled-up dog leads, etc. The guys at Merakai were keen to include a diverse range of characters in the label designs to reflect their brand ethos, and we really tried to include as much detail and pattern as possible so you might discover something new each time you look at the can.

Which of your labels are you most proud of?

EOP: All of the labels we have produced so far, but our favorite is How's Your Head Hun? for a number of reasons but mainly because this beer is a commentary on mental health that we want to act as a conversation-starter—plus, Olly and I are on the can together. We hope that all our beers are conversation-starters with their names, from I Licked It So It's Mine to How's Your Head Hun? we like to tell a story, have fun, and bring people with us.

What role do your visual identity and beer labels play in the success of your brand?

EOP: Merakai Brewing Co. is about creating meaningful connections and creating a community of like-minded people who can be their authentic selves and feel included. By creating labels with illustrations of every-day people, we hope that those people can see themselves and feel that they have found their tribe. The beer label itself expresses our point of view while standing out on the shelf, which is so important, as it's getting increasingly competitive.

Can you name two breweries whose visual styles you admire?

Oliver Parsons: I like a diverse range of image styles. Mainly photography, graphics, and typography. Bissell Brothers and Northern Monk: Patrons Project are sights to behold. EOP: I enjoy cans that tell a story, have a distinct style, and are a bit surrealist. Lervig has an interesting point of view, and I also like Yoho Brewing's can artwork. ▲

> # We wanted to create labels that spark a conversation, that make people want to pick us up and have a look to see what we're all about.

EMMA O'NEILL-PARSONS
Co-Founder

WE'RE CONNECTED
AREN'T WE?
6% ABV – NEIPA

HOW'S YOUR
HEAD HUN?
4.7% ABV – HELLES

WE PUT OUR
LOVE IN THIS
6.5% ABV – BOSTON STOUT

Collective Arts Brewing

LOCATION
Hamilton, Canada

DESIGN
Bob Russell (Creative Director),
Ryan Thibault (Design Director),
various illustrators (see index)

A grassroots craft brewery, Collective Arts Brewing hands over their labels to artists across the world, resulting in a gloriously unpredictable visual identity that supports emerging artists and celebrates creativity.

How would you describe the visual style of your brewery?

Bob Russell (Co-Founder and Design Lead): Everything we do at Collective Arts has been done to keep our brand subservient to the work of the artists we collaborate with. Our whole story is built around finding and curating the work of emerging artists all over the world, and we keep this in mind in everything that we do. Our product is consistent while our visual style is ever-changing.

What is the process for designing the label for a new release?

BR: Our process for labels is actually a strategic system developed to work out a neutral structure for the art submission, selection, curation, and release. Once art from an artist is submitted, an outside jury chooses the pieces through an unbiased selection process. The artwork is then assigned to a beer that best matches the feel of the art. Artists are paid and retain full ownership of their work, an important mandate honored by Collective Arts.

Where does the inspiration for the labels come from?

BR: Our labels are sourced externally and since they change on such a frequent basis, the inspiration really comes from our brand narrative. Our core story of being the originator of merging beer and artwork on labels is what really drives our story. From the start, we have co-created our brand with artists. Collective Arts stays fresh and new, and reflects what's going on in the art community at the time.

Which of your labels are you most proud of?

BR: What we are really proud of are the special collections we have curated, as well as numerous collaborations with other breweries that we love and admire. Our Amplified Voices series has been one of our most important curations to date, a series of limited-edition art by a collection of BIPOC artists, which launched in March 2021. This curation challenged the status quo, featuring artists and artwork that convey a sense of hope for a safer and more inclusive future.

What role do your visual identity and beer labels play in the success of your brand?

BR: Our changing visuals are our identity. Our point of difference is how we approach the labels. When we first developed this system of putting artists on our labels, there were not too many beer brands giving up this type of real estate. We knew from the beginning that this was our chance to stand out. Collective Arts changed the way craft beer is presented and opened the gate to a world that seemed different and unrelated. This idea and standard is baked into our DNA; it is our purpose and we are honored to have paved the way for others.

Can you name two breweries whose visual styles you admire?

BR: It has been fantastic to watch how art has become the main way other breweries define their brands. There is a ton of creativity in how craft-beer brands are using their labels to communicate a message or convey a feeling. ▲

From the start, we have co-created our brand with artists.

BOB RUSSELL
Co-Founder and Design Lead

Left Handed Giant

LOCATION
Bristol, U.K.

DESIGN
James Yeo

Independence and creative freedom lie at the heart of Left Handed Giant's community-owned business. Their ingenious labels front progressive beers sold in a brewpub overlooking the floating harbor of Bristol.

How would you describe the visual style of your brewery?

James Yeo (Designer): The visual style of the brewery has always tried to be expressive, inviting, and constantly evolving, which matches what we try to do with our beers.

What is the process for designing the label for a new release?

JY: We as a brewery put out a wide variety of ever-changing beers, so we need to produce a lot of new label designs. Generally, we start with naming the beer, and once that's nailed down, I'll go away and draw up a design. Left Handed Giant is very good at giving me as much creative freedom as I want—there's nothing in terms of a brief to follow. As I look after this whole part of the brand, I have built in tropes or mainstays that exist as part of my artistic style and help to keep the brand looking consistent. Once the illustration is complete, I will insert it into a label layout and share it with everyone in the brewery for comments and checks. Then it gets signed off and goes to print. ▶

Where does the inspiration for the labels come from?

JY: I get a lot of inspiration from the media that I consume. I watch a lot of cartoons like *The Simpsons, Dragon Ball Z,* and recently I've been watching *Moomins* with my son. I also listen to a lot of music when drawing and spend a good deal of time looking at other illustrators online. I'll take things from all these areas and work them together to influence what I'm doing.

Which of your labels are you most proud of?

JY: I'm in two minds when it comes to which designs are my favorite. There are classic labels that I love, like Dream House, but also a stream of new labels like the recent Spiralling Prism label that I also love. Generally, the latest design I've put together that I feel pushes my illustration style forward is my new favorite.

What role do your visual identity and beer labels play in the success of your brand?

JY: Visual Identity and label design play a big part in the success of our brand—it's probably second only to the quality of the beer we produce. When we first started out, we were using a very straightforward, safe graphic design style that I don't think fit with what we were trying to accomplish, and it wasn't helping us reach new audiences. It made it hard for us to stand out in a crowded market-place. So we moved from that to what we have now, at the same time as moving from cuckoo brewing to owning our own brewhouse, and we have continued with this illustration-based identity since then.

Can you name two breweries whose visual styles you admire?

JY: Breweries whose visual style really resonates with me are Hudson Valley in New York and Floc. in Margate, Kent. ▲

Visual identity and label design play a big part in the success of our brand—it's probably second only to the quality of the beer we produce.

JAMES YEO
Designer

DREAM HOUSE

HAZY PALE ALE
5.9% ALC VOL

HOPS
CITRA CRYO, GALAXY, MOSAIC, VIC SECRET

ALLERGENS: CONTAINS: BARLEY, OATS, WHEAT /INNEHOLDER
BYG, HAVRE, HVEDE / INNEHÅLLER / KORNMALT, HAVRE,
VETE / INNEHOLDER / BYGGMALT, HAVRE, HVETE / ENTHÄLT
GERSTE, HAFER, WEIZEN / CONTIENE / CEBADA, AVENA,
TRIGO / CONTIENT / ORGE, L'AVOINE, BLÉ
BEER, STARKÖL, ØL, BIER, CERVEZA, BIÈRE

BREWED AND CANNED BY:
LEFT HANDED GIANT, BRISTOL, UK
EU ADDRESS:
100% COLD CHAIN, AVE DE CHÂTILLON
73000 CHAMBÉRY, FRANCE

440ML ℮

BEST BEFORE SEE BOTTOM
BÄST FÖRE SE BOTTEN/BEST FÖR SE BUNN

WOODLAND CREATURES

PISTACHIO & HONEYCOMB STOUT
6.9% ALC VOL

ADDITIONS
LACTOSE, PISTACHIO, HONEYCOMB

440ML ℮

THE WORLD WAS MY IDEA

HAZY DOUBLE IPA
8.0% ALC VOL

HOPS
MOSAIC CRYO, MOSAIC T90, MOSAIC INCOGNITO

440ML ℮

OH DEAR THAT DIDN'T GO TOO WELL.

CHEESEBURGER CAVALRY

INDIA PALE ALE
6.9% ALC VOL

HOPS
CITRA CRYO, MOSAIC

440ML ℮

WORLD IN MOTION

FRUITED GOSE
4.5% ALC VOL

FRUIT
PASSIONFRUIT, TANGERINE
ADDITIONS
SMOKED SEA SALT

BREWED IN COLLABORATION
WITH OUR FRIENDS AT
DROP PROJECT

440ML ℮

New Hokkaido

LOCATION
Montana, USA

DESIGN
Sally Morrow Creative

ILLUSTRATION
Emile Holmewood

New Hokkaido

ニュー北海道

KODAMA DOUBLE IPA
THE ANCIENT TREE YOU JUST WALKED PAST—
DOES A TREE PHANTOM LIVE THERE? IS IT
MARKED WITH A SACRED ROPE? SAY HELLO,
AND BOW TO A WISE AND VERY OLD FRIEND.

16 FL OZ (473ML) • ONE PINT • ALC 8.5% BY VOL

New Hokkaido

ニュー北海道

YAMABIKO RICE LAGER
WAIT, DID YOU HEAR THAT? THAT MOUNTAIN
ECHO THAT TOOK TOO LONG? SHOUT AGAIN.
NOW LISTEN. THE YAMABIKO ARE ANSWERING
YOU, SOMEWHERE UP ON THAT SNOWY PEAK.

16 FL OZ (473ML) • ONE PINT • ALC 5.0% BY VOL

With design inspired by childhood fairy tales and Hokkaido's bewitching landscapes, New Hokkaido merges the traditions of Japanese brewing with Montana's innovative craft beer scene.

How would you describe the visual style of your brewery?

Sally Morrow Creative (Designers): New Hokkaido Beverage Co. is a phantom brewery, everywhere and nowhere. By remaining flexible about where brewing happens, they hope to create new possibilities in beer making in the U.S. and Asia.

What is the process for designing the label for a new release?

SMC: Research and strategy at the beginning of every project has led to our design inspiration and storytelling. We've pulled from the stories our client heard as a child in Japan. The fairy tales about supernatural entities called *yōkai*— each with their own purpose of creating good luck, mischief, or harm—have provided a wonderful springboard for our design ideas.

Where does the inspiration for the labels come from?

SMC: Our inspiration came from lots of research. Stories about *yōkai* provide both ancient and modern visual interpretations, and are prolific in Japan. The island of Hokkaido, Japan, is close to our client's heart—a land of jagged mountains, deep snow, and pristine forests—and is also where the brewers obtain the rice that goes into their beer making. We have lots of creative stories to pull from as the beer varietals are created.

Which of your labels are you most proud of?

SMC: We truly love each of them for different reasons. We're proud of the line of New Hokkaido seltzers because they innovate in that category. Each can includes a story about its *yōkai* and our unique visual interpretation. Typographically we had fun creating a structure that made room for varying name and copy lengths, all on bright pop color palettes. The combination of shiny and matte finishes adds extra interest to the can.

What role do your visual identity and beer labels play in the success of your brand?

SMC: The 360-degree wrap of the illustration on the beer labels creates a unique look for each of the labels and packaging overall. Each tells its own story essentially, and the "sliding screens" contain the brand identity, typography, and storytelling. The impact of these beer labels has been phenomenal at retail and on social media.

Can you name two breweries whose visual styles you admire?

SMC: Mikkeller and Modern Times, because of their innovative and creative ideas. Both breweries value people, have fun, and demonstrate a strong commitment to good design. ▲

ニュー北海道

New Hokkaido

HE HAS NO ARMS. HE HAS NO LEGS. HE HAS NO BODY. AND JUST LOOK AT THOSE EYES! WHY DID DARUMA SIT FACING A WALL FOR NINE LONG YEARS? EXACTLY.

A PHANTOM BREWERY. EVERYWHERE AND NOWHERE NEWHOKKAIDO.COM

DARUMA
INDIA PALE ALE

16 FL OZ (473ML)
ONE PINT
ALC 6.5% BY VOL

Fonta Flora

LOCATION
North Carolina, USA

DESIGN
Colin Sutherland/Woolly Press

With an emphasis on seasonal flora and local ingredients, Fonta Flora brings English tradition and Belgian inspiration to the Appalachian Mountains.

How would you describe the visual style of your brewery?

Colin Sutherland (Artist): I would describe Fonta Flora's style as heavily illustrative. We also favor strong minimal design and a playful approach to typography and hand-lettering. Fonta Flora produces a lot of different beers and different styles, so I would like to say that our aesthetic keeps pace with the beer side of things while maintaining an overall sense of cohesiveness.

What is the process for designing the label for a new release?

CS: This can vary drastically between beers, but typically once a beer is scheduled, we will either brainstorm illustration/design concepts and names as a team or someone will have a particular idea from the start. I will then go off and produce a draft and send it back to the team for review. We will then go back and forth revising until it's right.

Where does the inspiration for the labels come from?

CS: All over. Again, Fonta Flora makes so many beers you have to find inspiration everywhere just to keep up. The most common sources are from the ingredients themselves and the flora and fauna around us. Fonta Flora places incredible importance on the quality, sustainability, and locality of their ingredients. We also take great pride in these old mountains we call home and find inspiration from every inch of them and the critters that also call them home.

Which of your labels are you most proud of?

CS: I'm particularly partial to the You've Changed/We've Changed series and Steinbock and Steinfest. For the more type-focused labels I really like Old Man's and Nebo Pilsner.

What role do your visual identity and beer labels play in the success of your brand?

CS: I think our visual identity is crucial in setting us apart in a very crowded market. Like elsewhere in the world, small-batch craft beer has exploded in the markets we operate in, and many breweries have come and gone. Art has an immeasurable effect on attracting consumers and ensuring they become repeat customers.

Can you name two breweries whose visual styles you admire?

CS: The Veil and Oxbow are the obvious two. I'm lucky to call Tim Skirven (from The Veil) a friend and his work is so rad—beautiful and dark but still light enough to be refreshing. He's such a talented illustrator and a great designer. I don't know the folks at Oxbow, but if you love typography and you love beer, you need to check them out—they're the best in the business. ▲

> # The most common sources of inspiration are from the ingredients themselves and the flora and fauna around us.
>
> COLIN SUTHERLAND
> *Artist*

YOU'VE CHANGED

an unfiltered double
india pale ale dry-hopped
with galaxy, citra,
mosaic and talus cryo

1 pint   8.5% alc/vol.

Brewed and Canned at
Fonta Flora Brewery
Nebo, North Carolina

Fonta Flora
BREWERY

0 710859 925378

Old Man's

WEST COAST PILSNER BREWED WITH
CITRA, MOSAIC AND HBC 692 HOPS

1 PINT 5.2% ALC./VOL
FONTA FLORA BREWERY
NEBO, NC

0 710859 925316

Fonta Flora
BREWERY

Des Cantons

LOCATION
Québec, Canada

DESIGN
Éric Chouteau/Sans Cravate

EIPA

6·5% ALC./VOL.

TONS

BIO

PIC DE C L'OURS

ALE BLONDE

4·7% ALC./VOL.

DES CANTONS

BIO

DANS L'VENT

BLANCHE-HEFEWEIZEN

4·5% ALC./VOL.

DES CANTONS

Located in a region dense with mountains, forests, and lakes, Des Cantons take inspiration from sport and the great outdoors for their action-packed labels.

How would you describe the visual style of your brewery?

Junior Maheu (Owner): Unique and fun. Most of our labels/beers are about sport, being outdoors, and enjoying life, so we aim to keep it all fun, make people smile, and not take life too seriously—although our beers are very serious and of great quality.

What is the process for designing the label for a new release?

JM: My brewer, David Plasse, and I decide on a beer style that we wish to make. Then I'm the one who comes up with the name and sport that I want to feature. It's a difficult task for which I consult with friends, family, co-workers, etc. When I'm set on a name and sport, I share my inspiration with Éric in a long conversation. Part of the reason I chose Éric, aside from his obvious talent, is the chemistry between us. Not only does he understand what I want, he often takes it to another, better level.

Where does the inspiration for the labels come from?

JM: We're from Orford, Québec, a known destination for outdoor activities; it's in our DNA. So far, we've featured hiking, alpine skiing, hockey, road cycling, running, kitesurfing, and mountain biking.

Which of your labels are you most proud of?

JM: For me it's Allez Pou-Pou. I just love the story behind it about Raymond Poulidor, the French cyclist who was the eternal second but the crowd's favorite because he was a nice, simple man. The inspiration for the name comes from the title of a video of him training on a major hill where he says, "After, we'll just have to drink a few cold ones…"

What role do your visual identity and beer labels play in the success of your brand?

JM: It plays a huge role! It's our identity that speaks first to the consumers. We have to show who we are, our brand's uniformity, and what the beer is about within a few seconds.

Can you name two breweries whose visual styles you admire?

JM: La Grange Pardue, who feature paintings by Marcel Fecteau all about the rural side of their region. And La Souche has a unique style—just beautiful. ▲

> # We have to show who we are, our brand's uniformity, and what the beer is about within a few seconds.
>
> JUNIOR MAHEU
> *Owner*

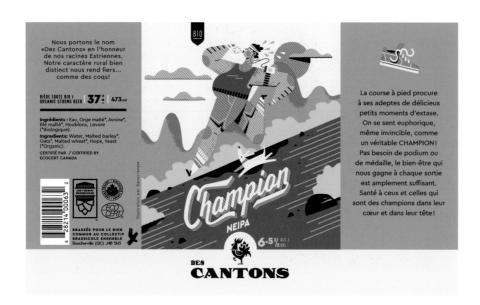

Nous portons le nom «Des Cantons» en l'honneur de nos racines Estriennes. Notre caractère rural bien distinct nous rend fiers... comme des coqs!

BIÈRE BIO / ORGANIC BEER | 13 | 473 ml

Ingrédients : Eau, Blé malté*, Orge malté*, Houblons*, Levure (*Biologique). Ingredients: Water, Malted wheat*, Malted barley*, Hops*, Yeast (*Organic).
CERTIFIÉ PAR / CERTIFIED BY ECOCERT CANADA

BRASSÉE POUR LE BIEN COMMUN AU COLLECTIF BRASSICOLE ENSEMBLE Boucherville (QC) J4B 5H3

DANS L'VENT
BLANCHE-HEFEWEIZEN

4.5% ALC./VOL.

DES CANTONS

Le kitesurf c'est la symbiose entre l'humain, l'air et l'eau. Rien ne sert de se battre contre les éléments, il faut plutôt les écouter et les ressentir pour ne faire qu'un avec eux. Le résultat est un mélange enivrant de surf et de voltige. Kitesurfer dans le vent n'est pas une chose facile, mais la sensation de voler qui l'accompagne est une récompense immense!

Nous portons le nom «Des Cantons» en l'honneur de nos racines Estriennes. Notre caractère rural bien distinct nous rend fiers... comme des coqs!

BIÈRE FORTE BIO / ORGANIC STRONG BEER | 22 | 473 ml

Ingrédients : Orge*, Blé*, Avoine*, Houblon*, Levure (*Biologique). Ingredients: Water, Malted barley, Oats, Malted wheat*, Hops*, Yeast (*Organic).
CERTIFIÉ PAR / CERTIFIED BY ECOCERT CANADA

BRASSÉE POUR LE BIEN COMMUN AU COLLECTIF BRASSICOLE ENSEMBLE Boucherville (QC) J4B 5H3

COWBOY
IPA BRUT

5.8% ALC./VOL.

DES CANTONS

Force est d'admettre qu'il faut être un peu cowboy pour rouler à vélo au beau milieu des arbres, sur un sol bourré de roches et couvert de racines! Chapeau bas à ceux et celles qui enfourchent leur monture pour cavaler dans les sentiers et fendre les trous de bouette!

Un esprit sain dans un corps sale. Allez, hue!

Nous portons le nom «Des Cantons» en l'honneur de nos racines Estriennes. Notre caractère rural bien distinct nous rend fiers... comme des coqs!

BIÈRE BIO / ORGANIC BEER | 30 | 473 ml

Ingrédients : Eau, Orge malté*, Blé malté*, Avoine*, Houblons*, Levure Kveik (*Biologique). Ingredients: Water, Malted barley*, Malted wheat*, Oats*, Hops*, Kveik yeast (*Organic).
CERTIFIÉ PAR / CERTIFIED BY ECOCERT CANADA

BRASSÉE POUR LE BIEN COMMUN AU COLLECTIF BRASSICOLE ENSEMBLE Boucherville (QC) J4B 5H3

Allez Pou-Pou
SESSION IPA

4.5% ALC./VOL.

DES CANTONS

Clin d'œil à Raymond «Pou-Pou» Poulidor (1936 - 2019), légende du cyclisme français, cette session IPA est destinée à tous les amateurs de vélo.

Bien que reconnu comme l'éternel deuxième des grands tours, l'accessible et sympathique Pou-Pou, était sans aucun doute #1 dans le cœur du public.

Nous portons le nom «Des Cantons» en l'honneur de nos racines Estriennes. Notre caractère rural bien distinct nous rend fiers... comme des coqs!

BIÈRE BIO / ORGANIC BEER | 25 | 473 ml

Ingrédients : Eau, Orge malté*, Blé malté*, Houblons*, Levure (*Biologique). Ingredients: Water, Malted barley*, Malted wheat*, Hops*, (*Organic).
CERTIFIÉ PAR / CERTIFIED BY ECOCERT CANADA

BRASSÉE POUR LE BIEN COMMUN AU COLLECTIF BRASSICOLE ENSEMBLE Boucherville (QC) J4B 5H3

Sweep
ALE ROUSSE

5.5% ALC./VOL.

DES CANTONS

À la fin de la journée de ski, les patrouilleurs sillonnent les pistes une dernière fois lors du sweep pour fermer la montagne. C'est alors que le terme après-ski prend tout son sens. Une bière rousse aux arômes maltés avec des notes caramélisées sur laquelle repose une mousse blanche. Un remontant qui n'est pas sans rappeler les couleurs officielles de la Patrouille canadienne de ski.

Nous portons le nom «Des Cantons» en l'honneur de nos racines Estriennes. Notre caractère rural bien distinct nous rend fiers... comme des coqs!

BIÈRE BIO / ORGANIC BEER | 15 | 473 ml

Ingrédients : Eau, Orge malté*, Houblons* Levure (*Biologique). Ingredients: Water, Malted barley*, Hops* Yeast (*Organic).
CERTIFIÉ PAR / CERTIFIED BY ECOCERT CANADA

BRASSÉE POUR LE BIEN COMMUN AU COLLECTIF BRASSICOLE ENSEMBLE Boucherville (QC) J4B 5H3

PIC DE L'OURS
ALE BLONDE

4.7% ALC./VOL.

DES CANTONS

Vieille de 400 millions d'années, la chaîne de montagnes des Appalaches s'étend à perte de vue dans le paysage estrien. Se trouvant sur le fameux sentier des Crêtes, le pic de l'Ours est le deuxième sommet en importance du Parc national du Mont-Orford. En le gravissant, vous serez récompensé par un point de vue spectaculaire de 360° sur la région !

Annex Ale Project

LOCATION
Calgary, Canada

DESIGN
Daughter Creative

Harnessing Alberta barley and mountain-fed water, Canada's Annex Ale Project produces experimental and seasonal brews paired with wryly witty copy.

How would you describe the visual style of your brewery?

Annex Ale Project and Daughter Creative: Annex Ales and our seasonal range under the Annex Ale Project brand both have an artistic appeal, with a slightly subversive tone. From the unexpected twists of our can art, to the complex and gently biting tone of our copy, we are here to probe the world's existential angst and relieve some of the anxiety with great beer.

What is the process for designing the label for a new release?

In our seasonals, the beer style influences both the design and color choices. Each can has a fixed type system for the name, style, ABV, etc. on the can front, and a brand bar around the back that allows space for long copy—a feature of our brand. Our can art consists of a baseline drawing with abstracted colored shapes over the top to add depth and visual interest. Tints of the colors used in shapes are used as background floods to differentiate each release on the shelf and cue the flavors of what lies within.

Where does the inspiration for the labels come from?

Our line drawings and shapes are highly influenced by the beer style. King's English—our Earl Grey and lemon ale—has a stylized, steaming teacup, abstracted tea leaves, and a gentle shade of blue—a reference to ornate Delftware teacups. Color is a cue for flavor as well, with bright citrus and berry pops on our sours and deep browns on our coffee stout and milk chocolate stout.

Which of your labels are you most proud of?

Our self-deprecating celebratory beer Pity Party is a great indication of our design system and our values in general. The simple line drawing of a beautiful gift and the joyful pink bubbles are sharply undercut by the sarcasm in the copy as we attempt to celebrate during a global pandemic. It's a can that makes anyone want to pick it up and drink it, with copy that makes our true brand zealots laugh to themselves as they sip—the perfect blend.

What role do your visual identity and beer labels play in the success of your brand?

The visual sophistication and softness of the label design combined with the biting wit of the copy means our beer has shelf appeal, and then a deeper message and storytelling that keeps our fans coming back. We have a point of view on the world, and our design system allows us to express that in a slightly subversive way, while still being aesthetically appealing and flavor- and style-forward. Our cans are cohesive on the shelf, and the design system is efficient and very scalable, letting us release shorter runs of experimental styles—something our progressive audience is always enthused by.

Can you name two breweries whose visual styles you admire?

Bellwoods Brewery in Toronto and Hudson Valley Brewery in Beacon, New York. Both breweries do a phenomenal job of creating their own visual worlds and characters, and successfully use their can aesthetics to tell stories. This visual world helps create a narrative for their esoteric beer names. As a consumer, it feels as though both have fun with their visual style and pay attention to brand consistency while exploring a wide range of design. And the beer is delicious too. ▲

Our can art consists of a baseline drawing with abstracted colored shapes over the top to add depth and visual interest.

ANNEX ALE PROJECT
AND DAUGHTER CREATIVE

Fuerst Wiacek

LOCATION
Berlin, Germany

———

DESIGN
*Imelda Ramović/
Mireldy Design Studio*

Each can of Fuerst Wiacek beer is an artwork designed to match the adventurous liquid inside. Based in Berlin since 2016, the brewers draw inspiration from New England and German brewing styles for their own flavorful creations.

How would you describe the visual style of your brewery?

Imelda Ramović (Designer): The main idea of the Fuerst Wiacek brewery is to make creative beers that offer our consumers a combination of carefully selected quality ingredients from which they can create new beer experiences. So our aspiration was to design a label to convey that passion in making beer and to tell the story of each individual beer. For each new beer, a visual story is always created in a unique way, and the artwork is never repeated.

What is the process for designing the label for a new release?

IR: Beer ingredients, the name of the beer, and whether it is a collaboration or not are the starting points in creating labels. Then a visual story is created based on these basic parameters.

Where does the inspiration for the labels come from?

IR: In most cases, the name of the beer itself is the basic inspiration for the motif. Our goal is to illustrate different experiences to further enrich the sense of pleasure that these beers provide us.

Which of your labels are you most proud of?

IR: It's always hard to pick one because each design has its own story. But if I really had to choose, it would be Airhead, Discotheque, Metz, and Jejune.

What role do your visual identity and beer labels play in the success of your brand?

IR: Good branding gives added value to the product, makes it more competitive in the market, emphasizes brand values, and conveys a clear message about brand values. I think our labels successfully convey the clear idea, vision, and passion that Fuerst Wiacek has as a brand.

Can you name two breweries whose visual styles you admire?

IR: There are really a lot of interesting visual solutions in this category. If I had to single out two, it would be Mikkeller and Halo. ▲

> ## Our goal is to illustrate different experiences to further enrich the sense of pleasure that these beers provide us.
>
> IMELDA RAMOVIĆ
> *Designer*

With designs that can feature anything from fire-breathing dragons to far-off planets, Cloak & Dagger's eye-catching labels draw inspiration from graffiti and subway art.

How would you describe the visual style of your brewery?

Leigh Pearce (Creative Director at Lolly Studio): Fun, playful, bold, and graphic. Some might say odd. I set out to produce cans that you want to pick up and handle.

What is the process for designing the label for a new release?

LP: It all starts with the name. The names of the beers are abstract and not descriptive in terms of style, strength, or color. The name is essentially the platform for the illustration. Once I have a clear image in my head, I roughly draw out a few digital layout options and work on a color scheme. I use these as a loose guide within the design package and tighten up the art using geometric shapes and the restrictive use of 45-degree angles.

Where does the inspiration for the labels come from?

LP: There's no easy answer for this. It might come from hearing a lyric or reading a line from a book or just from muttering my own rhymes walking to and from the studio. Whatever's in my head at the time is spewed out into Adobe Illustrator. The bold style of the artwork is influenced by graffiti. I often use dots, broad strokes, highlights, and light flares, albeit in a vectorized format, all techniques employed by subway-art legends. Most designs are character-based, which is a core element of my illustration style.

Which of your labels are you most proud of?

LP: I'm generally into the label that I'm working on at the time. That said, I'm still into Audacious Facelift (although I will probably change it slightly the next time we brew it).

What role do your visual identity and beer labels play in the success of your brand?

LP: As a relatively new, pretty small cuckoo brewery, we needed to stand out in an increasingly saturated market, both in fridges and on shelves, as well as in people's minds. We've achieved this locally with our interesting beer naming, use of language, vibrant color palettes, striking artwork, and personality. So I'd say our brand vision has been a major asset in launching our brewery. It also helps that our beer is incredibly delicious.

Can you name two breweries whose visual styles you admire?

LP: I try not to look within the industry as I find it can be stifling, but I really like North Brewing Co.'s style. They use minimal color palettes in a similar way to us, but with a simplistic design focus that never feels dated. ▲

> It all starts with the name. The names of the beers are abstract and not descriptive in terms of style, strength, or color. The name is essentially the platform for the illustration.

LEIGH PEARCE
Creative Director

Mothership

An all-female collective that champions women in craft beer, Mothership is leading a new wave of brewing and drinking with a social conscience.

How would you describe the visual style of your brewery?

Jane Frances LeBlond (Founder and Art Director): The Mothership visual style is intended to be strong and confident but also thoughtful and considered. We cover some sensitive topics in the stories behind our beers, and we try to reflect these in our can designs for special releases. We rely on an overall visual style for recognition, rather than slapping our logo over everything.

What is the process for designing the label for a new release?

JFL: Generally, our special releases fall into two categories: our Extraordinary Women series where we celebrate women who have not necessarily been recognized for their achievements and our Volume series where we react to issues that concern us. For the Extraordinary Women series, we spend quite a bit of time researching and deciding who to feature, then we work with a fantastic illustrator called Erin Aniker who creates the portraits. The Volume series is a bit more varied; it's done a lot by sense and intuition. I try to react to how the issue makes me feel and create a design in response.

Where does the inspiration for the labels come from?

JFL: I try not to be inspired by things I see in the beer industry but get my inspiration from life around me, from my senses, from everything I see. I do not like to conform to standard beer-can design rules, but to make my own based on how I feel it needs to look to deliver the message I want it to.

Which of your labels are you most proud of?

JFL: All of them! The core can labels really stand out and the illustrations by Atelier Bingo are outstanding and super-fun. I love the illustrations by Erin Aniker in the Extraordinary Women series, and together as a set they

look really strong. And our Volume series labels are very close to my heart as they are a representation of how I feel in that moment.

What role do your visual identity and beer labels play in the success of your brand?

JFL: I think our visual identity plays a strong part in our success. When we first started, the intention was to create a brand that looked like it had always been around. We did this quite successfully and people are still surprised to learn we're only two years old. We get a lot of compliments on our can design, and they are strong in a fridge or pump line-up.

Can you name two breweries whose visual styles you admire?

JFL: As a designer, one of the things that enhances my experience of drinking beer is beer-can design. A bit like records and record sleeves, I enjoy drinking a beer and looking at the can design. I love the illustrations on the Wild Card cans: they're beautiful, surreal, and they draw you in. I can get really lost in them, and the beer is outstanding too. I also think Duration do a great job with their cans, their photography is really nice, and they do some brilliant promo videos. I also really love the Canopy designs—they're such fun, as beer should be! ▲

Beak Brewery

LOCATION
Lewes, U.K.

DESIGN
Jay Cover

After several nomadic years, Beak Brewery has put down roots in East Sussex, U.K. They brew unfiltered, seasonally inspired beers with unmistakable, primary-colored labels.

How would you describe the visual style of your brewery?

Daniel Tapper (Founder): Minimal, playful, and oblique. Jay Cover's work is seemingly very simple. But look closely and you'll notice all kinds of quirks and references that are not always immediately obvious—we like to think our beer is a little like this too!

What is the process for designing the label for a new release?

DT: We never ask Jay to design his work around the beer, because the risk is the work will feel too forced. Instead, we look through his portfolio and pick out things that we think look cool. It's just about what looks good. He'll then riff off this to create a new piece of work. The artwork is as important as the beer, so we'd never expect it to be led by what's in the tin.

Where does the inspiration for the labels come from?

DT: The illustrations often have zero connection to the beer name—a little bit like our brewery logo. Some people probably think, "What the hell?" but we like this approach because it gets the synapses firing! It basically comes down to what looks good and what makes us smile.

Which of your labels are you most proud of?

DT: I'm a really big fan of the label Jay did for Wool, our DIPA collaboration with Northern Monk, which depicts a big ball of twine. The idea was to indirectly evoke Leeds's proud wool-making heritage. It's colorful, fun, and it directly evokes the sweetshop flavors of the beer. I also love the label for Lulla, which shows a couple hugging. It came out mid-lockdown when we were all missing a bit of human contact, and I think that's what our customers like about it.

What role do your visual identity and beer labels play in the success of your brand?

DT: I think it's really important. Although the quality of our beer is our number-one priority, the visual identity is what has to grab people's attention in the first place. I don't really see the point of putting out great beer and then considering the artwork as an afterthought. That said, our branding isn't to everyone's taste, but that's totally fine.

Can you name two breweries whose visual styles you admire?

DT: The Kernel would be my number-one choice. It's iconic, DIY, and utilitarian, and it says so much about the brewery in such a nuanced way. And I love everything about the Sierra Nevada Pale Ale label, from the slightly kitsch painting to the hand-drawn font. It just perfectly captures both California and the brewery's humble roots. It's so good that they've never changed it. ▲

> # The artwork is as important as the beer, so we'd never expect it to be led by what's in the tin.
>
> DANIEL TAPPER
> *Founder*

BEAK

WURL! | RASPBERRY SOUR 4%

BEAK

Belief | IPA 6.5%

BEAK

Power | Vienna Lager 5.2%

BEAK

OOPLA | IMPERIAL STOUT 10%

BEAK

AMBLE | IPA 6.5%

Beak x Northern Monk

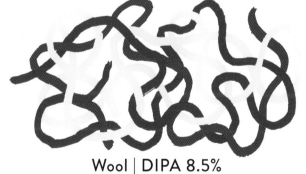

Wool | DIPA 8.5%

BEAK

POPPLE | PALE 5.5%

Beak Brewery

Pool | Pale 5%

Gamma Brewing Co.

LOCATION
Herlev, Denmark

DESIGN
Leif Gann-Matzen

Conceived by five craft beer-loving friends, Denmark's Gamma is an innovative microbrewery with a tendency toward the lavish use of hops and sleek, playful designs.

How would you describe the visual style of your brewery?

Coy Eakes (Co-Founder and Creative Director): In a broad sense I can say we lean toward a minimalistic and clean presentation. I'll let Leif explain more about the artwork.

Leif Gann-Matzen (Artist): I tend toward imagery that's a mixture of psychedelia and science, sometimes interlaced with cultural references if the name calls for it. Usually it ends up being a bit enigmatic, which hopefully opens up the interpretation.

What is the process for designing the label for a new release?

CE: Usually it starts with a name. Sometimes I'll explain the inspiration but usually Leif just runs with it. He works up a few images, and we make selections based on that. Then that gets attributed to a beer, sometimes with intention but usually not. The order of operations on all of that can vary or be completely backward.

Where does the inspiration for the labels come from?

CE: From the name side, sometimes it's some crazy word Anders Jensen (Co-Owner) has found that we just think is absurd. Often it's based around scientific concepts, dystopian woes of the digital age, rap references, or just some obtuse wordplay or reference that sounds funny.

LGM: It usually comes directly from the name, but I rarely start out with a very clear idea about what the imagery will be, and sometimes it's totally unrelated. Often I'm discovering through the process of making.

Which of your labels are you most proud of?

CE: We asked the rest of the Gamma team and we got a nice list: Blow Pop, Jewel Net of Indra, Big Doink, Superstudio, Beep Boop, Mesh, and Rotunda. Big shout-out to Svend Sømod who does some guest design work for us and is also responsible for undeniable favorites Freak Wave and Iterate. Honorable mention to Extra Natural and Gamma Kølsch. These are special because it took a lot of development and care to emulate a traditional beer label style while adding our own spin.

Can you name two breweries whose visual styles you admire?

LGM: Omnipollo and Stillwater. ▲

Alefarm Brewing

LOCATION
Greve, Denmark

DESIGN
Kasper Tidemann

Located just south of Copenhagen, Alefarm Brewing is a tight-knit, family-run brewery with a focus on modern hoppy offerings, farmhouse ales, and full-bodied stouts. The bucolic scenes and watercolor paintings wrapped around their cans are a testament to their Nordic roots.

How would you describe the visual style of your brewery?

Kasper Tidemann (Founder and CEO): I would describe it as open, rustic, and authentic. My ambition is for the visual style of Alefarm Brewing to always be welcoming and in tune with our Nordic heritage. For this reason, I like to use watercolor, open field imagery, and rustic brushes to create and cultivate the Nordic vibe that I feel our visual style has.

What is the process for designing the label for a new release?

KT: Every beer that we brew goes through a process that begins with us giving a name to the beer. The name of the beer is what decides the style of the artwork. Our beer names can be dreamy, esoteric, or contain cultural and historical references to famous artists. From that starting point, the label design process begins.

Where does the inspiration for the labels come from?

KT: I find my inspiration in contemporary art, writings, music, and more.

Which of your labels are you most proud of?

KT: I would probably have to say the Signature Series from Alefarm Brewing. The label artwork is based on watercolor depictions of abstract imagery, historical figures, and landscapes. I particularly like this series of labels because of their rustic and authentic appearance.

What role do your visual identity and beer labels play in the success of your brand?

KT: Our visual identity is key to our brand identity as a whole. It depicts who we are as a company, as people, and as a culture. It's the foundation upon which our brand is built and all our beers—along with their label designs—play a vital part in this story. ▲

Celestial Beerworks

LOCATION
Texas, USA

DESIGN
Molly Reynolds

The labels on Celestial Beerworks's brews are an ever-shifting display of cosmic phenomena and art through the ages—a fitting complement to the Dallas brewery's ever-changing line-up of beers.

How would you describe the visual style of your brewery?

Molly Reynolds (Co-Founder and Creative Director): Our brewery focuses on combining space-y imagery, scientific themes, bold colors, and interactive art. We want to surround our patrons with design, imagery, and visual interest. I am constantly adding to and changing the designs in the taproom, and I try to keep the style fun and light-hearted. I like to make the space busy but not overwhelming, which matches well with many of our beer styles in which a lot is going on but in a balanced way.

What is the process for designing the label for a new release?

MR: We generally have two or three beer releases every week. Usually this means I have to pump out multiple label ideas each week.

Sometimes I get a burst of inspiration and am able to design some labels ahead of time, and sometimes I have to come up with the name first and force a label to match it. I try to keep my color palette somewhat consistent, but within that boundary, I like to vary my methods. I tend to combine graphic design, photoshop, photography, and painting. This allows me to keep it fresh for customers, match the particular beer style, and have freedom for myself when inspiration strikes.

Where does the inspiration for the labels come from?

MR: It is nice to have the overarching space, science, and art themes to tie (most) of all the ideas together. There is never a lack of cosmic phenomena or art-history themes to pull from. We also love to connect our ►

labels to childhood nostalgia and to current events and trends. I try to create bridges between our social media with the taproom and cans as well. We have done interactive polls in which people's answers have shown up in our can imagery, raffles in which the winner gets to choose who to picture on the can, and a design contest for local artists to have a chance to showcase their work on our cans.

Which of your labels are you most proud of?

MR: Hopception. It was out of my comfort zone and more concept-driven. I felt like it brought the atmosphere of the taproom and the layered nature of the particular beer into the art really well. It made for a really cool photo shoot as well, allowing us to take a photo within a photo within a photo. I also really like my Cancel Culture label. There was so much meaning behind it, being a nod to the current social phenomenon while including imagery of female octopi (who murder their partner after mating) and ancient sculpture.

What role do your visual identity and beer labels play in the success of your brand?

MR: There are some pretty unique benefits in being the artist behind the taproom design of Celestial as well as designer of the can labels. I am able to keep the imagery and colors cohesive and connect all the themes. We want to bring the same atmosphere and experience of our taproom to those sipping our beers at home. Just as we ensure the beer inside the can is consistent with that on tap, I want to make sure the designs are similar to those in our physical space. This has been especially crucial this year with so many people unable to venture out and enjoy time in local businesses.

Can you name two breweries whose visual styles you admire?

MR: Left Handed Giant in the U.K. and Hudson Valley Brewery in New York. I haven't been to either location (yet!) but love their aesthetic from afar (that's the beauty of social media). I am a huge fan of the wild, funky, surreal imagery on the Left Handed Giant labels, and I really admire the simplicity and the calm, gentle beauty of the Hudson Valley labels. ▲

> **I like to make the space busy but not overwhelming, which matches well with many of our beer styles in which a lot is going on but in a balanced way.**

MOLLY REYNOLDS
Co-Founder and Art Director

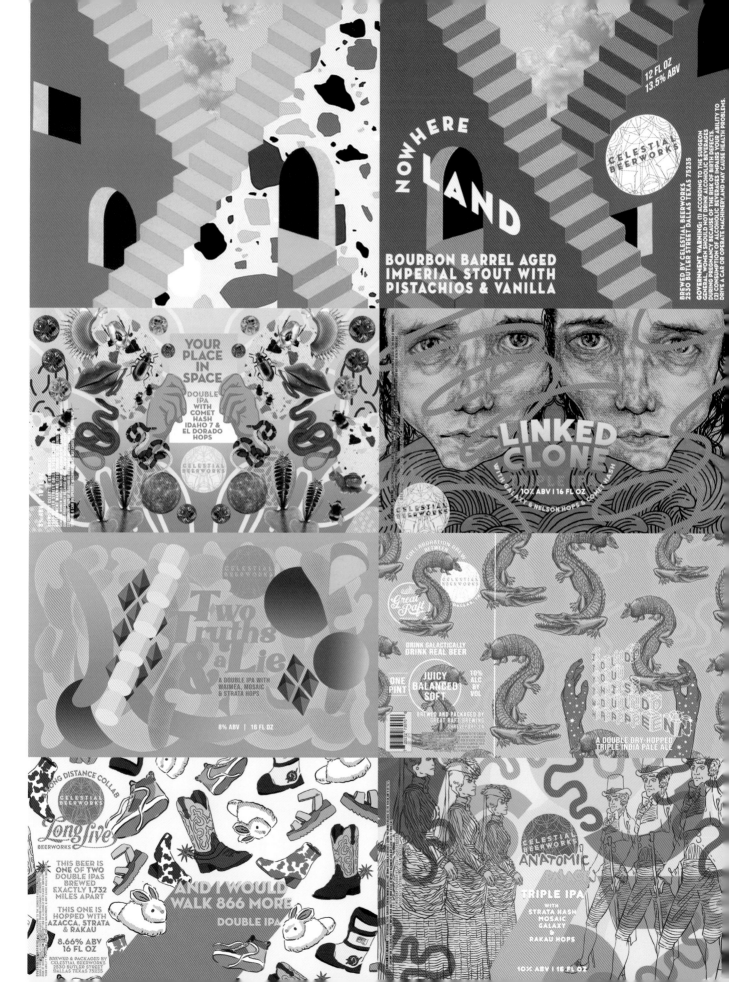

Dieu du Ciel!

LOCATION
Québec, Canada

DESIGN
Classics: Thaïla Khampo
Creations: Bénédicte Pereira Do Lago
and Pierre-Antoine Robitaille

With over two decades in the business, Dieu du Ciel! is a venerable brewer of bold beers. Last year, the Québecois brewery gave their image a total revamp to better reflect their inclusive values and dedication to innovation.

How would you describe the visual style of your brewery?

Leïla Alexandre (Brand Director) and Bénédicte Pereira Do Lago (Graphic Designer): In November 2020, we underwent a complete visual overhaul and went from what could be described as a gothic/abbey-beer-inspired style to a more poetic and dynamic one that remains authentic to what defines us. Our Classiques line is illustrated by local Québecois artist Thaïla Khampo, whose poetic, colorful, and refined style perfectly represents our flagship beers. Our Grands Classiques line features historical illustrations by Yannick Brosseau, whose paintings evoke timeless myths.

What is the process for designing the label for a new release?

New releases are mostly part of our Creation line, which is the segment where our brewers can experiment with new styles or brew a beer style they really like and think is worth rediscovering, such as our brown ale Castelnau. We like to reflect this experimentation on the can labels, which leave space for the illustrators to express themselves.

Where does the inspiration for the labels come from?

The DDC! team mostly brainstorms to find a name, and then our design department looks for talented local artists whose work we love and whose style we think will fit well with the beer. They are free to do whatever the name and beer style inspire in them. The labels are also sometimes done by the DDC! design team. For the Creation category, to date we have worked with Piece of Paper, Aless MC, Teenadult, Célia Marquis, and Pierre-Antoine Robitaille. ▶

Which of your labels are you most proud of?
Rosée d'Hibiscus for the strong link between the former label and the new one. The transition works very well, and the consumer can really recognize this one on the shelves, even if they're unaware that Dieu du Ciel! went through a whole rebranding process.

What role do your visual identity and beer labels play in the success of your brand?
The need to update and standardize the company's image has been felt for several years. Our old logo had tiny characters and fine lines that were hard to read. Our new logo is purposely more luminous and bolder. We also wanted to distance ourselves from a certain religious imagery and some representations of women on a few of our labels that felt outdated and at odds with our values. The changes will improve the visibility of our products on the shelves and standardize our appearance in retail spaces so that consumers can easily recognize them and make better-informed choices, while remaining true to our identity.

Can you name two breweries whose visual styles you admire?
Robin Bière Naturelle for their colorful, minimalistic, and delicate labels made by Jason Cantoro, a Montreal-based artist. And Brasserie Dunham for their eclectic approach—they work with a different illustrator or artist for almost every new label they create. It makes their brand unique and diversified. Simon Bossé is an excellent art director. ▲

The DDC! team mostly brainstorms to find a name, and then our design department looks for talented local artists whose work we love and whose style we think will fit well with the beer.

LEÏLA ALEXANDRE
Brand Director
BÉNÉDICTE PEREIRA DO LAGO
Graphic Designer

DISCO SOLEIL

IPA AUX AGRUMES — CITRUS IPA

BLANCHE DU PARADIS

BLANCHE DE STYLE BELGE — BELGIAN-STYLE WIT

IMMORALITÉ

AMÉRICAINE IMPÉRIALE — AMERICAN IMPERIAL

Põhjala

LOCATION
Tallinn, Estonia
—
DESIGN
Marke Saaremets

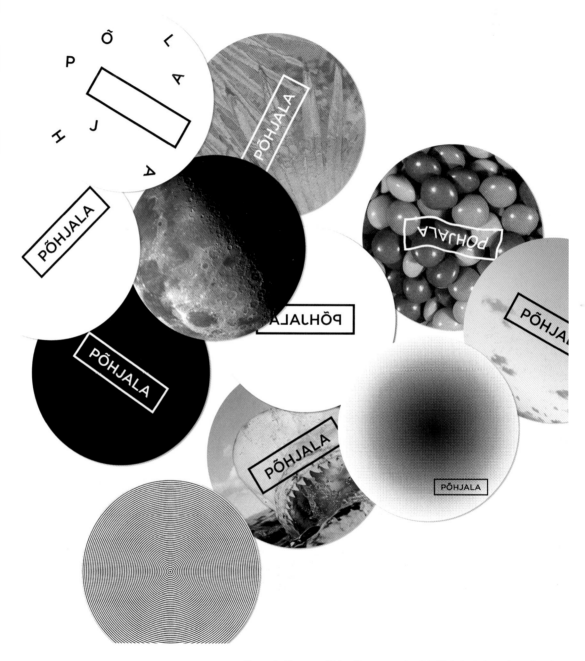

Translating as "Northern realm," Põhjala takes inspiration from Estonia's nature, culture, and cuisine. Their singular methods include long barrel aging and beers brewed with rare botanicals and forest ingredients.

How would you describe the visual style of your brewery?

Marke Saaremets (Designer): Põhjala's visual style is about having a distinctive and memorable look that links to our beers, local culture, and nature.

What is the process for designing the label for a new release?

MS: It consists of two integral components—the beer and its name. If these are set we proceed with the visuals. Our brewmaster, Chris Pilkington, supplies me with hints of the beers' characteristics.

Where does the inspiration for the labels come from?

MS: Inspiration mostly comes from the elements mentioned above, but also knowing that we (and the craft beer industry as a whole) are very open-minded about what to have on the label.

Which of your labels are you most proud of?

MS: The first that come to mind, in random order: Kirg, Torm, Prenzlauer Berg, As Good As it Gets, Mets, Õhtu, Baltic Pride.

What role do your visual identity and beer labels play in the success of your brand?

MS: I hope it plays a role in the success, but I can't judge that.

Can you name two breweries whose visual styles you admire?

MS: If I had to pick, probably Stillwater and To Øl for their multifaceted visuals. ▲

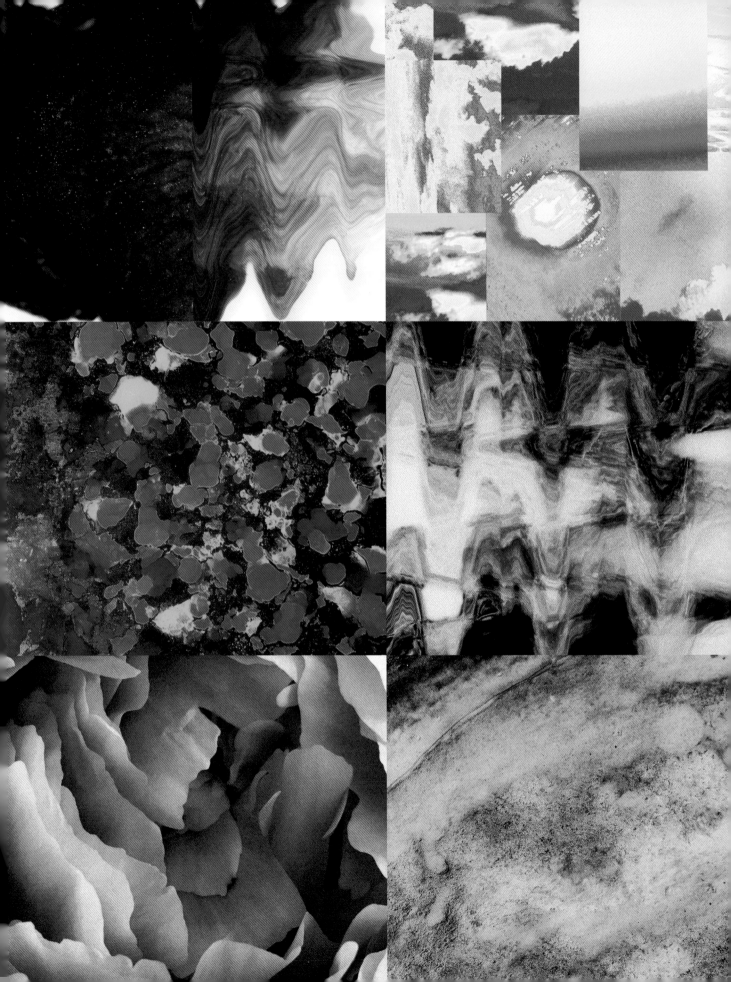

To Øl

LOCATION
Svinninge, Denmark

DESIGN
Kasper Ledet

Offbeat Danish brewers To Øl draw on a constellation of pop culture references and underground ephemera to label their potent, provocative, fresh, and floral beers.

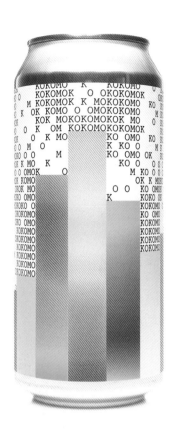

How would you describe the visual style of your brewery?

Kasper Ledet (Art Director): Referential, inconsistent, idiosyncratic, and slightly eccentric. Once in a while the planets and stars align perfectly and unexpected beauty emerges.

What is the process for designing the label for a new release?

KL: A controlled crash of tight deadlines, conversations, doubt, and occasional megalomania. PDF files going back and forth in what can sometimes feel like an eternity.

Where does the inspiration for the labels come from?

KL: One-hit wonders, obscure pop songs, British techno clubs of the 90s, Italian avant-gardes, Per Kirkeby and the rest of the gang from Eks-skolen, corporate branding, generic annual reports, contemporary graphic design, Niels Bohr, Lars von Trier, airports, the dark side of modernism, and peripheral architecture.

Which of your labels are you most proud of?

KL: The label for Hazy DC NEPA: painting, bad Photoshop effect, or the view through a frosted window?

What role do your visual identity and beer labels play in the success of your brand?

KL: The artworks hopefully serve as a way to visualize the abstract experience of drinking a beer. We very much think of the design as an integral part of the product and not just as functionalist communication.

Can you name two breweries whose visual styles you admire?

KL: Omnipollo—an extraterrestrial Swedish psychedelic dream—and Amager Bryghus for keeping it real! ▲

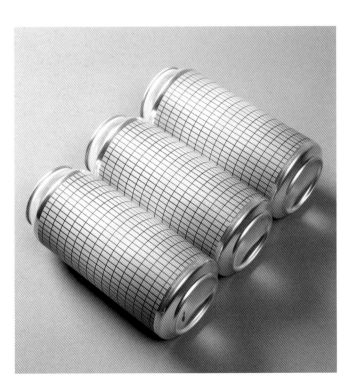

Garage Beer Co.

LOCATION
Barcelona, Spain

—

DESIGN
Sevkan Ariburnu/Acreb Studio

Pioneering the New England beer revolution in Spain, Garage Beer Co. conjures hoppy brews with poppy visuals in the heart of Barcelona.

How would you describe the visual style of your brewery?

Sevkan Ariburnu (Designer and Art Director): Superrealism meets pop.

What is the process for designing the label for a new release?

SA: One, getting the monthly brew schedule. Two, deciding on the overall visual direction. Three, selection of material and creative planning. Four, execution and retouch! If I have a work overload, Sergio Ävila helps with photography. And once in a while we love to spice things up by adding illustrations on our cans. Silustra (Silvana Casuccio) helps us with that.

Where does the inspiration for the labels come from?

SA: The brewery team, the bar pre-COVID, Barcelona, world current affairs, creative conversations around the globe, and my own personal experiences.

Which of your labels are you most proud of?

SA: My perspective on this question has changed over the years. Rather than being proud of one label, I am proud of the continuous and consistent work I've been putting into all of them.

What role do your visual identity and beer labels play in the success of your brand?

SA: I will leave that question to the Garage team to answer! I do my best to motivate the brewery team by making the cans shine bright on the shelves. At the end of the day, it's the brewers who make the beer delicious. I take my hat off to them.

Can you name two breweries whose visual styles you admire?

SA: Difficult question! I've always liked Deya, they're fun. But I keep discovering new stuff— BDQ Beer Co. is a good find. ▲

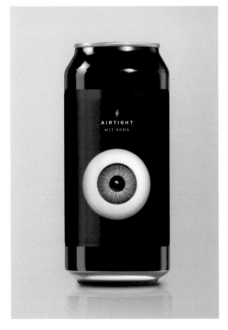

Brasserie du Bas-Canada

LOCATION
Gatineau, Canada

DESIGN
Alexandre Mercier

Known for its hopped-up creations and decadent stouts, western Québec's Brasserie du Bas-Canada was founded by two beer enthusiasts intent on bringing quality craft beers to their Outaouais region.

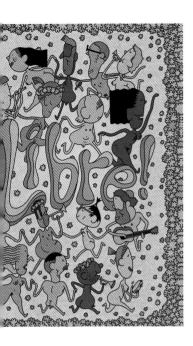

How would you describe the visual style of your brewery?

Alexandre Mercier (Designer): Although we hire several artists to illustrate our labels, I've illustrated a good majority of them myself. My style is a mix between digital collage and a textured vector approach.

What is the process for designing the label for a new release?

AM: The process begins with good graphic research, the search for an interesting concept, the sketch, and finally the digital illustration working with Photoshop and Illustrator. I will sometimes do up to five different visuals before I am satisfied.

Where does the inspiration for the labels come from?

AM: My inspiration comes from several sources. Social media of course, photography, video games, movies, and everyday life.

Which of your labels are you most proud of?

AM: We are very proud of the work by our various artists. Each has their own unique style. As for my personal work, Dryade and Océanides are among my favorites.

What role do your visual identity and beer labels play in the success of your brand?

AM: Branding and labels play a very big role in the success of our company. From the start, we wanted to have unique visuals that stood out on shelves and on social media. We are also very proud to showcase the work of local artists.

Can you name two breweries whose visual styles you admire?

AM: Not an easy choice, but I would say Bellwoods Brewery in Toronto and Messorem Bracitorium in Montreal. Bellwoods have a good consistency both in terms of branding and the design of their labels—an excellent balance between design and illustration. Same thing for Messorem—the visual unity is excellent. Messorem also stands out with their superb merchandise. ▲

Archetype Brewing

LOCATION
North Carolina, USA

DESIGN
Sean Jones/Humid Daze

With bold beers that reflect their vibrant surroundings, West Asheville's Archetype Brewing has a mission to collaborate creatively and support their local community.

How would you describe the visual style of your brewery?

Brad Casanova (Owner): Archetypes by their nature are defined and stimulating, and so must our labels be. We use sharp lines and bold colors to clearly convey concepts without words. Our Shoulder Devil label required a deep-red background, so there's no question you were warned before purchasing this high ABV hop dream. The Explorer label features dense foliage, and by bringing the foreground in, you become immersed in the jungle with a first-person perspective scene. Our design, graphics, and even the obligatory haikus are all meant to connect the drinker to the liquid therein. Such a daring feat requires boldness!

What is the process for designing the label for a new release?

BC: The process for each label is different, which keeps the creative process fun. It often starts with the beer, as making the decision to package a product often occurs after a beer has been brewed, named, and enjoyed by many on draft. Our beer development process is very open and we welcome input from staff. We keep a beer-name board in the office for all to contribute to. We once created a beer and label completely inspired by a recurring dream one of the bartenders was having. It's aptly named Will's Dream and the label is a pastel-laden scene showing a music festival, some lost sunglasses, and a pink-flamingo lawn ornament. We are also currently working with our designer Sean Jones to go in the opposite direction and start with the label first. Jones has created the label and chosen his moniker, Humid Daze, as the name for the beer. We now have the unusual challenge of making a beer worthy of his visual concept.

Where does the inspiration for the labels come from?

BC: We find situational imagery that evokes emotion or invites connection. When developing a label, we typically have the name and the tasting notes for the beer. Using those sensory elements helps bring us to a memory of ►

something, and from there we pull in imagery and color. Sometimes it's as simple as wanting to highlight the many plant-based elements of our Talking to Plants witbier. The ginger, coriander, orange peel, and wheat in this beer are all balanced but prominent, so the label shows a farmer in their field talking to the plants (it's good for them).

Which of your labels are you most proud of?
BC: Cowboy Poet is definitely a crowd favorite, it won USA Today's Best Beer Label for 2020. The lazy desert scene with a cloudy pink sky perfectly matches the drinking style of the lager. Some labels contain relatable immersive scenes (Timely Surrender shows a relenting swimmer floating in water) and some are completely farcical (Lunar Effect has a creature worshiping in the light of a smiling moon).

What role do your visual identity and beer labels play in the success of your brand?
BC: We rely on our labels to make a connection with the consumer. The label for Cowboy Poet is a great example. Cowboy poetry, a combination of artistry and tradition, is the perfect analogy for a craft lager. The label and graphics bridge that gap and unearth the layers present in our branding. It's up to the customer to choose how deep down the wormhole they want to go!

Can you name two breweries whose visual styles you admire?
BC: Many years ago I was a huge fan of Rogue. Their printed glass bombers were high-quality and amusing. Lately I've been loving Modern Times. The colorful and simple geometric patterns are eye-catching. ▲

Archetypes by their nature are defined and stimulating, and so must our labels be.

BRAD CASANOVA
Owner

North Brewing Co.

LOCATION
Leeds, U.K.

DESIGN
James Ockelford/Refold

A brewery that grew from a legendary music-loving bar, North Brewing Co. fuses art and musical references into bold, modernist labels.

How would you describe the visual style of your brewery?

James Ockelford (Designer): Modernist and minimal. Bold, bright, and rarely printed out of more than two pantone inks.

What is the process for designing the label for a new release?

JO: Before starting I tend to lay out all of the references in front of me: What type of beer is it? Is there a backstory to its existence? Is the label for a collaboration? Are there any visual cues to be taken from the collaborator's logo or branding? I select a soundtrack for the piece of work and then I go about creating. Each label tends to exist as a poster design first then gets adapted for the can label. I usually create several designs for each label, different layouts and different color schemes.

Robert (my brother) works with me and uses 3D rendering software to create quick mockups of the various designs. The winning design is then prepared for print.

Where does the inspiration for the labels come from?

JO: Music and art play a big role in inspiring designs. Before North Brewing Co. came into existence North Bar had been running in Leeds for 20 years. For me this was the best bar in the world—good beer, great staff, interesting clientele, and great music. You could sip Belgian beers while listening to the likes of Can, Aphex Twin, Radiohead, Tortoise, Ornette Coleman, and Philip Glass. Very left-of-center. Very interesting. I like to think the spirit of North Bar in the early 2000s plays a role in inspiring the design. ▶

Which of your labels are you most proud of?

JO: It almost always tends to be the most recent label I've been working on. But looking back over the last year I have to say I was very happy with how Into the Merzbau turned out. Not just the design, but I love the name and concept behind it. I'd like to think it may have introduced at least a few new people to the work of Kurt Schwitters (and possibly the work of Merzbow as well).

What role do your visual identity and beer labels play in the success of your brand?

JO: A key role. There are a lot of breweries producing a huge amount of beer. A strong, memorable identity has never been more important.

Can you name two breweries whose visual styles you admire?

JO: I'm a big fan of Highland Park Brewery in Los Angeles. I love the stories the labels illustrate, and there's a strong, joyful aesthetic. The other brewery I truly admire is The Kernel, they never bend in their simple, to-the-point approach to packaging. In a visually noisy beer world, they're a breath of fresh air. That brown-paper label is the guarantee of quality. Would I like the design as much if the beer wasn't excellent? I don't know. Other breweries whose work I genuinely love include Deya, Brew Your Mind (in Hungary), To Øl, and Dig Brew—their earlier glass-bottle labels especially. ▲

Music and art play a big role in inspiring designs.

JAMES OCKELFORD
Designer

Modist Brewing Co.

LOCATION
Minnesota, USA

DESIGN
*Tyler Mithuen, Ebby Pruitt,
Wes Winship, Run the Jewels*

Located in North Loop, Minneapolis, Modist Brewing Co's custom brewhouse enables them to defy the rules with gloriously unorthodox brews. Their visuals are equally nonconformist, pulling from a kaleidoscopic range of influences and original art.

How would you describe the visual style of your brewery?

Tyler Mithuen (Director of Brand Development): The visual style of Modist is simply not limiting ourselves to one thing. Our goal is to always be modifying and evolving, always trying to be on the cutting edge of the industry's creativity and ideas of what a brand identity is. We have a one-of-a-kind brewhouse that allows us to be very creative in the beer-making process, and the feel and look of the brand are meant to reflect that. Each brand of beer has its own look and feel, which helps reflect the uniqueness of the liquid inside the cans.

What is the process for designing the label for a new release?

TM: Just like the looks of the labels, the process can look different for each can. Most often, it starts with a name that helps give way to a vision in the head of either Keigan Knee (our Co-Founder and Director of Product Development a.k.a. Flavor Overlord), me, or whoever came up with the name. We then create a mood board to help designate how we want the brand to feel, the style we want to convey, and different elements we think will help create a compelling visual experience. After that we figure out if it's best suited for me or an outside artist. From there, the designing begins with a few back-and-forths between the marketing team here and the individual designing the label, modifying it until the final product is achieved.

Where does the inspiration for the labels come from?

TM: Sometimes it comes from an artist's personal style and other times it comes directly from our brain holes. We've pulled inspiration from video games, music, movies, anime, comic books, and even Lego builds. We try not to limit how we're inspired when creating brands. The more we're open to seeing the world as a possible inspiration, the better our brand will grow and evolve.

Which of your labels are you most proud of?

TM: One of my favorite labels that we created with an outside artist is called Apiary Drip, a collaboration with our friends at Dangerous Man Brewing. The label was created by a super-talented artist named Ebby Pruitt. I think the Fruit City series (a design collaboration with Wes Winship and myself) and Death Sauce are some favorites that I have created, but the one I am most proud of was the beer we made with Run the Jewels. It was a fun collaboration with the hip-hop duo to celebrate the song they created for *Cyberpunk 2077.*

What role do your visual identity and beer labels play in the success of your brand?

TM: The look and feel of our brand identity goes hand in hand with the success of the Modist brand. For most people, the first interaction with our brand is on the liquor store shelf or on their social media feed. Our goal is to stand out on the shelves and the feed. The ability to have free range to develop original art on all of our labels helps us tell a unique story for each beer.

Can you name two breweries whose visual styles you admire?

TM: I try hard not to pay attention to too many other breweries so that our brand doesn't begin to merge with their identity, but I really love the look and feel of Bottle Logic. The visuals are created by Emrich, a husband-and-wife duo, and their designs are visual masterpieces. I'm also a fan of everything that comes out of Humble Sea. Frank Scott Krueger has created a visually unique brand that never disappoints in the simplicity, creativity, and overall fun-ness of the designs. ▲

> **For most people, the first interaction with our brand is on the liquor store shelf or on their social media feed. Our goal is to stand out on the shelves and the feed.**
>
> TYLER MITHUEN
> *Director of Brand Development*

Hop Hooligans

LOCATION
Bucharest, Romania

—

DESIGN
Diana Barbu

Bucharest-based brewers Hop Hooligans combine a geeky attention to detail with a mischievous streak of nonconformity. Their goal? To "achieve hop bliss."

How would you describe the visual style of your brewery?

Cristian Mihai Dinu (Brewer): It all kind of starts from the name—Hop Hooligans—which we chose in order to state from the beginning that we don't plan on setting strict limits on what we're going to brew. We wanted to show that with the themes used for the labels, too. Most of them push a more-or-less hidden social message, or straight-up mischief. At the same time, we don't really take ourselves too seriously, so the style is playful and contrasty with a touch of texture.

What is the process for designing the label for a new release?

CMD: It all starts from the beer recipe, the nerdy science stuff that happens behind stainless steel tanks—trying to come up with the best hop combo for a DIPA or the tastiest combination of adjuncts for a luscious imperial stout. Starting from that, we usually have some ingredients that help us form that first spark of a visual identity, and then we try to find a name and theme that work around said ingredient. Usually with hopped-up beers we tread a more specific path, with our "Achieve Hop Bliss" slogan in mind. With a name and a main theme set, we pitch it all to Diana, along with a mood board and as much info as we can come up with. It's great that we understand each other so well, and she always manages to enrich those muddled bits that are running around in our heads.

Where does the inspiration for the labels come from?

Diana Barbu (Designer): The easy answer would be pop culture, but, again, we don't really limit ourselves. We delve into art, music, lots of literature and movies, historic events, even philosophy. ▶

Which of your labels are you most proud of?
DB: All of them have a special story, but for me personally as an illustrator the ones with the girls are closest to my heart—Heartbreaker, Bee With Me, Sencha, etc. For the Hop Hooligans crew and the customers, I am sure that Crowd Control, Chupacabra or Koschei spark more joy.

What role do your visual identity and beer labels play in the success of your brand?
CMD: It's really important to stand out in a fridge full of craft beer (from a sales point of view), and our designs always seem to catch the eye. Of course, they're pretty and colorful, but they also have a lot of elements that make you take a second, more focused glance, to really get the whole picture and maybe even see if there's something hidden between the lines. It's awesome that people recognize a Hop Hooligan beer without searching for the logo but from the artwork and the style. It's really something unique, and we're happy that Diana puts up with us this much, helping us create a whole identity that makes it easy to stand out in a crowd of so many other great breweries.

Can you name two breweries whose visual styles you admire?
DB: Partizan, Zakładowy, and iconic Mikkeller. I love their style for the clear and consistent visual identity and for the quirkiness and playfulness. ▲

With a name and a main theme set, we pitch it all to our designer Diana Barbu.

CRISTIAN MIHAI DINU
Brewer

Superflux

LOCATION
Vancouver, Canada

—

DESIGN
Matt Kohlen

An ever-evolving experiment in beer production and innovation, East Vancouver's Superflux matches their distinctive IPA-focused beers with eye-catching, color-drenched visuals.

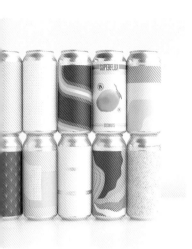

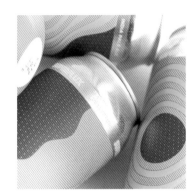

How would you describe the visual style of your brewery?

Matt Kohlen (Co-Founder and Brewer): Clean, approachable, impactful, evolving. My business partner, Adam, and I aren't afraid to constantly evaluate and adapt to what we think is cool and visually appealing. Our design taste continues to evolve as we're exposed to other creative people, teams, and projects.

What is the process for designing the label for a new release?

MK: We always start with the name and intention with said beer. We typically chat as a team and come up with an overall goal and feel of what we want the finished product to be. I basically design the label in my head over a few weeks or months, then move to the computer to execute. I'm big on the visualization side and growing an idea over time via seeing cool shit throughout the day.

Where does the inspiration for the labels come from?

MK: Mostly spotting cool stuff out and about. I take a lot of pictures and notes for ideas to be used in the future. For example, the Double Infinity Mosaic label is based on a can of paint we used during the brewery construction.

Which of your labels are you most proud of?

MK: Double Infinity Mosaic. It's super simple, clean, and bold, with sharp, classic colors. I love this design more and more as time goes by—it really achieves longevity through simplicity. We do a foil band around the edge of this label and most other core beers, which just adds a bit of class, consistency, and refinement.

What role do your visual identity and beer labels play in the success of your brand?

MK: It goes a long way. More so for people that are not familiar with what we do here at Superflux. The design definitely draws attention, and at the end of the day it hopefully introduces someone new to what beer really can be through our lens. From day one it has always been about the quality of product inside that can. And, fortunately, I think we have built a reputation over the years where people trust that the product in the can will meet or exceed their expectations.

Can you name two breweries whose visual styles you admire?

MK: Humble Sea is so cool and unique. Great use of white, hand-drawn elements, and color. Holy Mountain is simplicity and longevity done right. Clean, sharp, and memorable. ▲

Talea

LOCATION
Brooklyn, USA

—

DESIGN
IWANT

Pioneers in a male-dominated industry, Brooklyn's Talea was founded by two women entrepreneurs dedicated to offering approachable beers with fruit-forward flavors.

How would you describe the visual style of your brewery?

Talea: Our visual style is represented by our can and bottle labels, our taproom, and our digital presence. Common threads across all of these are layers and colors. In our taproom, our draft beers, served in glasses, are the feature, with a mix of textures like tile, brick, cement, and wood in colors like teal, pink, and terracotta creating a sophisticated backdrop. Our label designs prominently feature the beer name, style, and our logo layered on colorful geometric shapes with repeating themes.

What is the process for designing the label for a new release?

T: We select a beer style, build our recipe, and name the beer. When beers are on draft in our taproom, the name must stand apart because there is no label art. We provide designer John Gilsenan with the name, tasting notes, and specifics of the beer, such as a desire to represent a season, an emotion, or appeal to a specific occasion or type of customer. John presents us with a proof, and 75 percent of the time we have only fine-print notes (like changes in ABV or tasting notes), and we then approve.

Where does the inspiration for the labels come from?

T: Some of the label inspiration stems from the beer names, which are inspired by everything from the ingredients (Raspberry Crush is made with raspberry puree) to the emotion we want people to feel when they're sipping our beers—we wanted Brightside, a beer we brewed while fundraising to build our taproom, to inspire people and evoke optimism. Wheels Up was named after its Motueka hops from New Zealand, which would require a plane to visit. The circular rotation of stripes evoke the churn and whirring of an engine.

Which of your labels are you most proud of?

T: Sun Up Hazy IPA, our first beer. Sun Up's design set the tone for the visual identity of our brand: bright, playful, unexpected combinations—layers that entice your eyes and keep you exploring the design.

What role do your visual identity and beer labels play in the success of your brand?

T: Outside our taproom, you can find our beer at bars, restaurants, specialty beer shops, grocery stores, and high-end corner stores. We always wanted our beers to have their individual identity but still look like a family—which makes them stand out on the shelf. We believe the visual identity and branding have contributed to encouraging customers to grab our product off the shelves out of curiosity—the beer quality then convinces them to buy it again. Our labels and logos give customers an expectation of what they will experience in our taproom: a contemporary space with an inviting, engaging, and thoughtful beer-drinking experience. ▲

> # Sun Up's design set the tone for the visual identity of our brand: bright, playful, unexpected combinations.
>
> TALEA

Verdant

LOCATION
Penryn, U.K.

—

DESIGN
*James Wright, Ciro Bicudo,
Adam Robertson, AJ Higgins*

VERDANT

BREWING CO.

Brewed in a picturesque corner of Cornwall, Verdant's juicy, hoppy beers feature eccentric names dreamed up by staff and no limitations on their imaginative label designs.

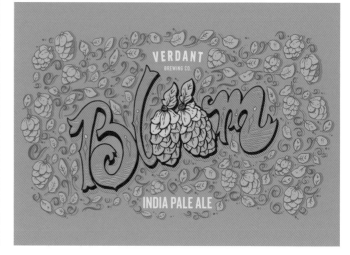

How would you describe the visual style of your brewery?

James Wright (Creative Design Manager): Eclectic! We like to be flexible with our approach to each beer, which lets us experiment and play with ideas. It also allows room for different voices and styles, and means we get to collaborate with interesting people. Most of all we just try to be creative and see where that leads us without confining ourselves to a single aesthetic.

What is the process for designing the label for a new release?

JW: It can vary, but more often than not we'll start with a spark of an idea that inspires a name. It might come from something unique or interesting about that beer, or it might come from somewhere completely unrelated. Once we've agreed on a name, it's over to the designer or artist to interpret that into a label design however they want. Sometimes there are specifics that need to be factored in (a detail, a color, etc.) but generally there are no limitations on design. We try to generate a few rough concepts to start, pick our favorite, and then go through a round or two of drafts before hitting the final design.

Where does the inspiration for the labels come from?

JW: We have a space where all our employees can throw in ideas: topical themes, personal thoughts, puns, jokes… The most fun ones to work on usually start from names that are emotive but open to interpretation, so when it comes to translating an idea onto the can there's space to take it to interesting or unexpected places. It can be much simpler than that, though. Occasionally a fully formed concept will drop into our heads and we just have to make it real.

Which of your labels are you most proud of?

JW: Out of the labels I've designed myself, probably Some Fifty for the sheer joy of working in that particular style and maybe Blended Blur for its purity. I also loved doing the illustration for Don't Fear the Ferryman. It's difficult to pick labels out though when we're always creating new ones. It's a transient process and time is often short, so the pride and satisfaction comes from expressing an idea succinctly and effectively.

What role do your visual identity and beer labels play in the success of your brand?

JW: First and foremost our success is built upon the quality of our beer, and our visual identity plays a vital role in how we connect people with it. Because our visual style is eclectic, we're not trying to define ourselves stylistically through a single aesthetic—we're simply always aiming for the best we can. I think communicating the continuity of this idea is the most important thing.

Can you name two breweries whose visual styles you admire?

JW: I've always had a soft spot for Keith Shore's illustrations for Mikkeller. But there are so many great designs out there it's hard to narrow it down. ▲

> ## Most of all we just try to be creative and see where that leads us without confining ourselves to a single aesthetic.
>
> JAMES WRIGHT
> *Creative Design Manager*

Unity Brewing Co.

LOCATION
Southampton, U.K.

—

DESIGN
Matt Canning

The positive, community-minded spirit of vegan-friendly Southampton brewers Unity Brewing Co. shines through in their lush pastel imagery.

How would you describe the visual style of your brewery?

Jimmy Hatherley (Founder and Head Brewer): We have a bright, modern feel with a hint of nostalgia. Our visual style represents our ethos of DIY, togetherness, and fun, with the illustrative style and signature of our in-house designer Matt Canning. We integrate our beer names into our label art and they always feature different characters and our distinctive pastel color palette.

What is the process for designing the label for a new release?

JH: We send the beer name, beer description, and a really short brief to our designer Matt Canning who comes up with a concept for approval. Once approved, we let Matt run with it.

Where does the inspiration for the labels come from?

JH: We get inspired by the beer style and name we've chosen, and we try to get that across in the artwork whilst keeping a fun, fresh, and vibrant look. Representing togetherness in our labels is always a focus as well.

Which of your labels are you most proud of?

JH: Our recent re-work of our core range really represents who we are as a company and gets the feel of the beers across well. Our latest collaborations with Queer Brewing and Elusive Brewing—Jupiter and Thinking With Portals, respectively—show our designer Matt Canning really getting into his stride.

What role do your visual identity and beer labels play in the success of your brand?

JH: It's the first experience anyone has of one of our beers, so we work hard to make sure they really represent our values. I think this helps people get an idea of who we are so they can connect with Unity before they've even opened the can.

Can you name two breweries whose visual styles you admire?

JH: James Yeo from Left Handed Giant does incredible illustrations with a unique look, and I think they're really fun. Thom Hobson from Deya is also awesome and so distinctive. Again, his artwork is fun and a little nostalgic, which we really like. They both have such an identifiable style—you can't help but enjoy it. ▲

Two Tides Brewing Co.

LOCATION
Georgia, USA

———

DESIGN
Alexandria Hall

The gorgeous psychedelic visuals of Two Tides Brewing Co. illustrate the sociable company's dedication to good beer, good conversation, and free pinball at their 41st Street taproom in Savannah.

How would you describe the visual style of your brewery?

Liz Massey (Owner and Marketing Director): Bright, welcoming, and sometimes a little weird.

What is the process for designing the label for a new release?

LM: We work closely with our illustrator, Alexandria Hall. It's a group effort every step of the way. Sometimes we have an idea in mind and let her know what we're imagining, but most of the time we just send her the beer name, and she sends us some sketches she thinks best represent it. We then pick our favorite sketch (and color palette) and go from there. We do a few reviews along the way while she's working and then go to print.

Where does the inspiration for the labels come from?

LM: About 90 percent of the time the label is inspired by the name of the beer and represents that in some shape or form. On our side, we pull from a lot of our favorite shows, movies, and music. Alexandria then bridges the gap from just a basic idea to the actual label that will represent the beer and our brand.

Which of your labels are you most proud of?

LM: Most recently Hot Commodity, Fluff Motif, Pure Space, and Too Tired to Dream.

What role do your visual identity and beer labels play in the success of your brand?

LM: It's everything. Especially in a world and industry so centered on social media and Instagram. Our visual identity directly impacts whether people visit our taproom and take beer home with them.

Can you name two breweries whose visual styles you admire?

LM: The Veil Brewing Co. and Burial Beer Co. I just love the unique styles of both of these brands, and they stand out. You can tell a beer is theirs without even seeing their logo on a can. Everything is creative, new, fresh, and they make you feel like you're a part of the excitement. They also do a great job of authentically representing their brand experience online. What you see online is what it's truly like when you visit in person. ▲

Play Brew Co.

LOCATION
Middlesbrough, U.K.

———

DESIGN
Alphabet

With fruity cartoon characters in retro wardrobes, the illustrations on Play Brew Co.'s labels are a nostalgic trip into 80s and 90s culture.

PLAY BREW Co

LONG WAVE

NEW ENGLAND PALE ALE 4.8%
CITRA & IDAHO 7

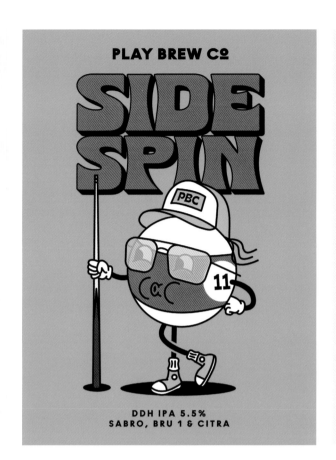

PLAY BREW C⁰

SIDE SPIN

DDH IPA 5.5%
SABRO, BRU 1 & CITRA

PLAY BREW C⁰

RASPBERRY & MILK
STICKY LOLLY
PALE ALE

5.5% ABV | STORE COOL DRINK FRESH | 440 ML

PLAY BREW C⁰

CHOCOLATE & HONEYCOMB
BIRTHDAY CAKE STOUT

6.5% ABV | STORE COOL DRINK FRESH | 440 ML

PLAY BREW C⁰

TROPICAL PINEAPPLE
FRUITY SOUR
GOSE

4.5% ABV | STORE COOL DRINK FRESH | 440 ML

How would you describe the visual style of your brewery?

Abbas Mushtaq (Co-Founder of Alphabet): Play Brew Co. is inspired by retro culture and nostalgia, so our branding and label follows suit. We're bold with color and have always believed in simplifying and cutting through the noise with our designs. Hopefully this comes across.

What is the process for designing the label for a new release?

AM: We work with Phil Layton from Play Brew Co. closely on label designs. We have quite a quick turnaround on labels and beers, which is also what makes the process great. We think about the flavors and hops of the beer and create a concept from there in terms of naming, color, typography, and illustration. For example, Baby Blue is a Blueberry Gose.

Where does the inspiration for the labels come from?

AM: A lot of retro packaging from the 80s and 90s, retro beer mats and the colors and typography associated with them. It also depends on the beer—for example, they have a flavored range of beers such as Raspberry and Milk Sticky Lolly, inspired by the drumstick sweets, so it made sense to look at the visual style associated with that.

Which of your labels are you most proud of?

AM: Lazy Daze and Double Dash will always have a place in our heart, as that's what Play Brew Co. launched with and they put the brand on the map. Personally speaking I really like Cherry Bomb as well, as it's simple and clean but still has a fun edge.

What role do your visual identity and beer labels play in the success of your brand?

AM: I think it plays a huge part. People interact with your identity and beer labels before they try it. First impressions count, especially in such a busy market, so it can't be understated how important our branding and labels are.

Can you name two breweries whose visual styles you admire?

AM: I really like Mikkeller and Camden Town Brewery from a design and branding standpoint. ▲

> # We're bold with color and have always believed in simplifying and cutting through the noise with our designs.
>
> ABBAS MUSHTAQ
> *Co-Founder of Alphabet*

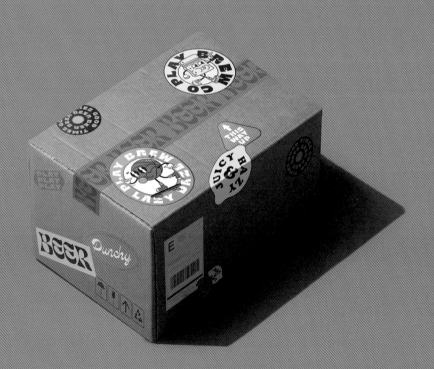

Amundsen

LOCATION
Oslo, Norway

———

DESIGN
Peter-John de Villiers

Oslo's largest brewery, Amundsen, creates swirling hand-drawn labels that evoke 60s West-Coast counterculture and the renegade spirit of surf and skate art.

ALL STACK · CHOCOLATE CHIP MAPLE COVERED PANCAKE – IMPERIAL PASTRY STOUT

How would you describe the visual style of your brewery?

Peter-John de Villiers (Artist): Everything is traditionally hand drawn with pen and paper, with a focus on vibrant colors, energetic line work, and a detailed finish. The artwork is reminiscent of skateboard, surf, and snowboard art and Fillmore-era concert posters…

What is the process for designing the label for a new release?

PJV: As the artist, I get the names and ingredients of the beer from Geoffrey Jansen van Vuuren at the brewery. Sometimes he comes with a suggestion for the artwork, and sometimes I play off the name. I start with a rough pencil sketch and then work up a finished illustration with pen and ink. I scan the drawings and color them in Photoshop. The artwork is sent off to the layout designer Lewis Ryan, and he puts together the text and label ready for print.

Where does the inspiration for the labels come from?

PJV: I fell in love with the aesthetic of skateboarding, snowboarding, and surfing, and it has inevitably had a big influence on my work. I try to put my own spin on it and make it fun to look at.

Geoffrey Jansen van Vuuren (CEO): We always try to give the beers names that would inspire our artist. It should be a continuous visual story from when you read the name of the beer to when you look at the artwork. ▶

Which of your labels are you most proud of?

PJV: It's hard to say, we've done so many at this point—I'm always looking forward to the next piece, I enjoy the process every time!

GJV: This is hard, we've done so many amazing artworks in the last seven years that it sort of feels like picking the favorite amongst your children. If I really have to pick one, I'll say Ink & Dagger. It's one of the first ones we did and the lines, detail, and color combinations just spoke to me. When I saw it, I felt our brand and what we stand for.

What role do your visual identity and beer labels play in the success of your brand?

GJV: Visual identities and brand recognition play a huge role these days. When there are so many breweries out there, it's important to stand out and be recognized. I have always believed if you can get the consumer to pick up your can and take a closer look, half the job is done. All you need then is to make sure the quality on the inside matches the expectations from the outside of the can. If you can master those two things, you are guaranteed to have a successful brand.

Can you name two breweries whose visual styles you admire?

GJV: I love the visual style and flow of Beavertown. Their design has always stood out to me. Taking their cans to the next level by implementing can-ends that match the designs is brilliant. KCBC has some of the best labels in the business. I love the playfulness in their beer names and the comic-book art style. ▲

> # Everything is traditionally hand drawn with pen and paper, with a focus on vibrant colors, energetic line work, and a detailed finish.
>
> PETER-JOHN DE VILLIERS
> *Artist*

PILLARS OF LIGHT — LEMON MILKSHAKE IPA

COSMIC UNICORN — BLACKBERRY & PEACH PASTRY SOUR

SUPER SANTA — CHOCO SHAKE STOUT

DOUBLE APOCALYPSE — DDH DIPA

Mountains Walking

LOCATION
Montana, USA

DESIGN
Sally Morrow Creative

ILLUSTRATION
Andrew Holder

Mixing a deep respect for ancient brewing traditions with an irrepressible curiosity and love of experimentation, Mountains Walking keeps their approach as wide-open as the landscapes of their Montana home.

How would you describe the visual style of your brewery?

Sally Morrow Creative (Designers): We'd describe the brewery as both contemporary in design and timelessly rustic. Love of the outdoors is reflected in the palette of wood grains and patterns throughout the brewery, mixed with large windows that let the outside in. The raw steel used in the bar and furniture mix with different wood grains and finishes, and the silver and copper brand identity colors appear as accents throughout.

What is the process for designing the label for a new release?

SMC: Research and client collaboration is key to providing the context for our design strategy. Our client, Gustav Dose, has put great trust in our design development—and from there we formulate ideas that become the springboard for design. Here's a quote from their brewer, inspired by a Zen philosophy for brewing beer: "Beer has been a human tradition for 10,000 years. When we engage this tradition with a beginner's mind, it opens the gate to boundless possibilities. This is how innovation happens."

Where does the inspiration for the labels come from?

SMC: For us, it comes from the minds of the designer and copywriter, who pull and develop ideas and stories that resonate. Our goal is always to surprise and delight consumers with our packaging. From there, typographic and illustrative possibilities are developed. Once we arrive at the design direction, an illustrator is chosen to develop the artwork specifically for the design, keeping in mind the communication of the story (including mandatory information), the space available on the can, considering paper/film/substrate, finishes, and the overall 360-degree shape of the package.

Which of your labels are you most proud of?

SMC: We're proud of the flagship Mountains Walking labels that wrap an abstract mountain scene around the can in different colorways for the different varietals—we love it especially because they bring to life the notion that "the mountains are walking" around the can (inspired by the Zen saying). The seasonal can designs are a favorite because each brings to life the name of the varietals, such as Opaque Thoughts and Chopping Wood.

What role do your visual identity and beer labels play in the success of your brand?

SMC: From what we've heard, the variety of designs under each brand umbrella have been well-received by customers. The beers are outstanding (as all who taste them find out), but the exciting visual styles have made a huge impact on repeat sales. Customers have posted on their social channels ways in which they've created a second use for cans (like herb and flower planters!), which is really gratifying.

Can you name two breweries whose visual styles you admire?

SMC: Halo Brewery and Captain Barley in São Paulo, Brazil. I love both of their approaches—as well as their exceptional design craft and visual innovation. ▲

> # The beers are outstanding (as all who taste them find out), but the exciting visual styles have made a huge impact on repeat sales.
>
> SALLY MORROW CREATIVE
> *Designers*

SEASONAL
WINTER SPRING SUMMER FALL
SERIES

DESSERT
CART

PASTRY STOUT
WITH HAZELNUT,
TAHITIAN VANILLA
AND COFFEE

FROM
MOUNTAINS WALKING
BREWERY

16OZ (1 PINT)   ALC 10.5% BY VOL

SEASONAL
WINTER SPRING SUMMER FALL
SERIES

CHOPPING
WOOD

SCHWARZBIER

FROM
MOUNTAINS WALKING
BREWERY

16OZ (1 PINT)   ALC 8% BY VOL

SEASONAL
WINTER SPRING SUMMER FALL
SERIES

CLOUD
CURTAIN

MOTUEKA OAT
WHIP IPA

FROM
MOUNTAINS WALKING
BREWERY

16OZ (1 PINT)   ALC 8% BY VOL

SEASONAL
WINTER SPRING SUMMER FALL
SERIES

SWEETS

BLUEBERRY LEMON
SOUR ALE WITH
VANILLA & LACTOSE

FROM
MOUNTAINS WALKING
BREWERY

16OZ (1 PINT)   ALC 5% BY VOL

Vertere

LOCATION
Tokyo, Japan

—

DESIGN
*Vertere and Taku Bannai
(Special Series)*

In the green western hills of Tokyo, Vertere makes beer as fresh and clean as the brewery's surroundings. Their cans are miniature art galleries featuring on-the-fly snapshots drawn from the brewers' travels.

How would you describe the visual style of your brewery?

Emile LeBlanc (Assistant Brewer): Our visual style is essentially based on simplicity. We use an especially minimalistic approach to our labels and brand. Pure white background, a square photo in the middle, and the least written text possible. The photos on our labels usually have little to no correlation with the beer inside the can, as we want people to enjoy the beer without any preconceived notions of what it will be like.

What is the process for designing the label for a new release?

EL: Our current process for designing a new label isn't overly complex. Basically, we choose a photo that we've taken, usually from our travels overseas, and fit it to our regular design. When we first started with this design though, we knew we wanted it simple, and we played around with varying sizes, placements, etc. for photos but settled on the one we have now, as we liked it best.

Where does the inspiration for the labels come from?

EL: Our main design was inspired by exhibits from art museums. Often when you go to art museums, paintings are framed on a blank wall to focus attention on the art. We thought we would try to replicate that on our beer cans. Plus, the ability to change the center photo while keeping the same design is a big bonus.

Which of your labels are you most proud of?

EL: Our Christmas 2020 labels are probably the ones I'm most proud of—a Christmas sour and stout. They're different from our regular design, and I think they capture, in an abstract way, some Christmas spirit, while still looking sleek. Out of our main series, our Magnolia label is one of my favorites. It's nothing more than a chair on a blue background, but it stands out well, and unless you look closely, you don't really realize what's going on at first. It was also one of our first can labels to be designed.

What role do your visual identity and beer labels play in the success of your brand?

EL: I think our labels and branding play a good part in the success that we've had here in the Japanese market. Although simple, our labels stand out quite nicely when lined up on store shelves, and they align well with the rest of our logos, merchandise, etc., so it's easy for the customer to understand and pick out our beer. Our design comes across very fresh and clean, and our goal is that the beer inside is as well.

Can you name two breweries whose visual styles you admire?

EL: Hudson Valley Brewery in New York State and Burdock Brewery in Toronto. These two breweries' visual styles share little resemblance to our own labels, nor do they really resemble each other. But Burdock has a fresh-looking, relatively simple design that we really like. Hudson Valley usually uses a much smaller, fine-detailed design, but that comes together on the can in a nice, eye-catching way to create a bigger picture. ▲

Overtone Brewing Co.

LOCATION
Glasgow, U.K.

DESIGN
Thirst Craft

In the Scottish craft beer scene, Overtone Brewing Co. stands out with the abstract art and visual illusions on their cans, inspired by underground club posters.

How would you describe the visual style of your brewery?

Kayley Barbour (Sales and Marketing Manager): We wanted to create a unique identity that stood out in bottle shops and reflected the quality and originality of our beers. So instead of having a similar design for every beer, we created a consistent system and layout to ensure brand recognition whilst largely contrasting the designs for each beer. When customers see this layout in a shop, it's easy to identify it's Overtone.

What is the process for designing the label for a new release?

KB: Every month I'll develop a brief with design references and a color scheme for a batch of beers due to launch the next month. Thirst Craft (Designer): We look forward to the Overtone brief every month, as it's never the same and allows creative freedom whilst building brand equity at the same time. We use the design references and brief that Overtone sends over, as well as the flavor profiles and style of the beer to influence the final pattern and design.

Where does the inspiration for the labels come from?

KB: Overtone is highly influenced by music, so initially our designs were inspired by soundwaves and movement. We take inspiration from a broad range of categories and ideas but always try to tie the design back to the name and beer style in some way.

We like to play with optical illusion and keep things pretty abstract. It's also important that they look tasty and appealing.

Which of your labels are you most proud of?

KB: Crystal Ball is one of our favorites; it's a big, special TIPA, and the design truly reflects that with an optical-illusion sphere using different shapes. Boogie Nights is another new release, which is a pornstar-martini-inspired sour beer. We briefed Thirst with some 70s designs, and they turned it into a fun, moving design.

What role do your visual identity and beer labels play in the success of your brand?

KB: We've successfully created an identity that stands out without having to make labels look the same. We don't stick to specific colors or designs, meaning every beer we create has its own visual identity. These make our beers more memorable to customers, as the designs stick in their head and maybe even encourage them to collect the cans and not miss out on any of our beers!

Can you name two breweries whose visual styles you admire?

KB: We all love North Brewing Co., as it has a similarity to Overtone with soundwaves and movement in their designs. Their labels always look so fresh and clean, much like their beer. All of us love Deya too. Their branding is so fun, unique, and creative. Every single label would look great on a T-shirt, on a glass, on a poster print—anywhere! ▲

Track Brewing Co.

LOCATION
Manchester, U.K.

DESIGN
Amy Haselden

Inspired by a two-year, round-the-globe cycling odyssey, Track Brewing Co. has put down roots in Manchester, but their polychromatic designs remain inspired by the wide world.

How would you describe the visual style of your brewery?

Amy Haselden (Designer): Colorful and experimental with playful gradients.

What is the process for designing the label for a new release?

AH: It starts with getting the beer details and name set up on the design and then—the best bit—I spend time playing around with colors, patterns, and shapes to see what I can make. For most designs I don't usually have a defined vision in my head before I start creating; I just like to go with the flow and play around with it.

Where does the inspiration for the labels come from?

AH: I like to take inspiration from the world around me; it's free and it's right there! Whether that's the gradient of a setting sky or the patterns of some funky tiles beneath my feet… Sometimes the colors are inspired by the flavors in the beers—making it look how it tastes. I also enjoy experimenting with different paper textures, negative space, etc. There is so much to explore—I'm excited by what's to come!

Which of your labels are you most proud of?

AH: I'd have to say the Digital Age collection, particularly Meet Me in the Middle, the collaboration with Range Brewing. The designs for the collection were initially just experiments I did during the lockdown, so it was really nice to be able to use them for labels too. The wavy design combined with the silver label was really striking and people seemed to love it. I think this collection paved the way for the visual identity that Track cans have, which is really cool.

What role do your visual identity and beer labels play in the success of your brand?

AH: I think the initial branding and labels were really strong and established Track well, so over the past few years, I've enjoyed developing this identity further by exploring the way that our cans look on the shelves. I feel like the labels have taken on their own identity and are now pretty recognizable as Track beers, which is awesome.

Can you name two breweries whose visual styles you admire?

AH: There are so many that I love, but one would have to be Range Brewing. The designs always look amazing, and I love the use of different typefaces for the titles. I was able to collaborate with their designer, Jess Vandersande, when they did their release of Meet Me in the Middle, and I love her work. Also Left Handed Giant's labels always look great—I love James Yeo's illustration style and each one is so wild and wonderful. ▲

FLOC.

LOCATION
Margate, U.K.

DESIGN
Illwookie/Will Richards

Community-driven brewery Floc. aims to build strong roots in the colorful British seaside town they call home. Their cartoony, laid-back visual style conjures good vibes and sunshine.

How would you describe the visual style of your brewery?

Ross Shields (Founder): I wanted the labels to be fun, colorful, and modern so they stood out on the shelves. It's such a crowded marketplace that for a small brewery like Floc. to succeed we needed a point of difference— hence the cut-out labels, which are tricky to set up and apply but are unique as far as I know. They change with every release, with a new die-cut made for each new label. Will Richards (Artist): I'd describe our art style as bold, cartoony, and fun. Our illustrations are often very character-based with an element of light-hearted humor.

What is the process for designing the label for a new release?

RS: Will designed everything from the start— logo, merch, etc. We change the illustration style every third or fourth release to keep it fresh. The label format doesn't change, so we can keep it consistent from a branding perspective. I send Will the name of the beer and let him work his magic.

WR: We try to mix up the composition of the artwork on the label. Each release of three or so cans has its own little theme and is always different, yet unmistakably Floc. This keeps things interesting for both the artist and the customer.

Where does the inspiration for the labels come from?

RS: The original mood board had a few references, Foam and Mikkeller mainly. Foam because of the cut-out nature of their labels and Mikkeller for their awesome artwork. At first we had just the Floc. logo at the bottom as a cut-out, which felt unbalanced. After a few trials Will came up with incorporating the artwork into the cut-out, and then it was just the challenge of finding a label supplier who could make them.

WR: It all boils down to the name of the beer.

Once we have that, we can mess around with wordplay and let our imaginations run wild!

Which of your labels are you most proud of?

RS: Easy Way Out is up there. It's a label version of a painting Will was working on at the time, and I love the way original art can be transferred to a can of beer and appreciated by a wider audience. Another one would be Unlimited Happiness, which sums up how Will and I work together. I sent Will the name and he came back with a frog in his underwear happily walking along holding flowers, and I thought... why not?

WR: My favorite is also our iconic happy frog in his underwear and socks. Unlimited Happiness was one of our earliest releases, and it encapsulates the feeling of the brand perfectly. The frog has since become our unofficial mascot. He is called Vinny for those wondering.

What role do your visual identity and beer labels play in the success of your brand?

RS: I'd say it's 99 percent of the success so far. To get noticed in the industry at our size is difficult. I wanted the brewery to look like an established brand straightaway—you only have one chance to make a good impression. The beer thankfully holds up to the branding, which was the aim from the start: great beer, great branding.

WR: Visual identity is often a customer's first interaction with a brand and entices them to taste the stuff. Of course, the beer then has to be delicious and Floc. has no troubles in that department.

Can you name two breweries whose visual styles you admire?

RS: Omnipollo and Mikkeller—they're visually stunning, consistent, and playful. At the end of the day, beer should be about enjoyment, fun, and positive vibes. That's what I'm trying to surround Floc. with, not only with the beer we make but the visuals created for it. ▲

Japas Cervejaria

LOCATION
São Paulo, Brazil

DESIGN
Yumi Shimada

Founded by three Japanese-Brazilian women passionate about brewing, Japas Cervejaria's unique recipes and design are inspired by the rich stories, aromas, and flavors of their joint cultural heritage.

AWĀ

― PEACH ―

07 IBU

SOUR ALE WITH PEACH

PURPLE
KAWAII
かわいい

6,4% vol
473 mL

60 IBU

ブラジル　　　日本
01
ICHI

BRAZIL · JAPAN
UM

45 IBU

How would you describe the visual style of your brewery?

Yumi Shimada (Co-Founder and Designer): Our brewery has a look that seeks to show the influence of Japanese culture in Brazil in a more contemporary and innovative way, breaking patterns and stereotypes of the traditional Asian look. We achieve this through the collage method, which always tells a story on each label.

What is the process for designing the label for a new release?

YS: We three founders always participate in the entire product-creation process by brainstorming together. Our company does not separate design and recipe: whenever we create recipes, we are already thinking of a name and concept. So we manage to have labels that are designed from the recipe to the execution of the art—they tell a complete story.

Where does the inspiration for the labels come from?

YS: Our labels are inspired by several factors: our Japanese-Brazilian mix in culture and cuisine, the history of our families who came here, and many artistic references that we like.

Which of your labels are you most proud of?

YS: In 2018, we created a beer marking 110 years of Japanese immigration in Brazil. We named it after the first ship that brought Japanese immigrants here, Kasato Maru. We chose a fruit that was also an immigrant in our lands, dekopon, a citrus that would go well with a NEIPA. Then we put it all together in a handcrafted label, using collage, to honor our ancestors.

What role do your visual identity and beer labels play in the success of your brand?

YS: Our visual identity has a super-important role for our brand, as it translates who we are as individuals in each product we create. That's why a lot of people can identify with us, because our labels show our ideals and also tell stories in a unique and innovative way, which draws attention even from those who don't like beer.

Can you name two breweries whose visual styles you admire?

YS: Mikkeller definitely manages to show its unique style with a super-modern and beautiful identity. We also love the Omnipollo labels— they are amazing. ▲

> # Our company does not separate design and recipe: whenever we create recipes, we are already thinking of a name and concept.
>
> YUMI SHIMADA
> *Co-Founder and Designer*

RIO DE
JANEIRO
MARU

6.5% alc.
50 IBU
473 mL

サワー
SAWĀ
PINK

07 IBU

WASA
ワサビール
BIIRU

5.5% alc/vol
1 Pint
45 IBU

ULTRA
SORACHI
空知王牌

6.8% alc/vol
1 Pint
30 IBU

SU
MO

alc/vol
IBU

サワー
SAWĀ
PLUM

07 IBU

YUZU
NAMA
BIIRU

18 IBU

NAMA
BIIRU

18 IBU

MATSU
RIKA

PILSNER WITH
JASMINE FLOWERS

3% alc/vol
1 Pint
27 IBU

BLACK
MATSU
RIKA
ジャスミン

DARK LAGER WITH
JASMINE FLOWERS

3% alc/vol
27 IBU

GOJAIRA

味噌
BLACK
MISO

11.5% alc/vol
1 Pint
68 IBU

サワー
SAWĀ
YUZU

4.1% alc/vol
1 Pint
07 IBU

SOUR ALE
WITH YUZU

KAWAII

KASATO
MARU
笠戸丸

5.5% alc/vol
40 IBU

AF Brew

LOCATION
St. Petersburg, Russia

DESIGN
Vasily WTF

AF Brew are pioneers of the Russian craft beer revolution. Housed on the former site of an 18th-century brewery, the company is inspired by more contemporary sources for their labels—pop culture, memes, and urban slang.

ABAUHAUS
URISTIC PASTRY SOUR WITH RUM BABA

How would you describe the visual style of your brewery?

Vasily WTF (Creative Director and Lead Designer): Simple shapes, bright colors, clear associations, and references to pop culture.

What is the process for designing the label for a new release?

VWTF: We always start from the recipe to check what references the ingredients might have. Then we look at the beer name. After the name comes the visual element of the label. So: ingredients, name, and art add up to the complete story.

Where does the inspiration for the labels come from?

VWTF: From the surrounding world and how it works. Also pop culture, movies, video games, urban slang, internet memes, and other stuff like that.

Which of your labels are you most proud of?

VWTF: I can't choose. Let's say that I make every label with care so I won't be ashamed of it later.

What role do your visual identity and beer labels play in the success of your brand?

VWTF: Maybe it sounds trivial, but visual identity makes our beer distinctive and recognizable among other beers and breweries. We have our own recognizable style of naming and art.

Can you name two breweries whose visual styles you admire?

VWTF: It's so hard to choose only two, but I'll go for To Øl and Prairie Artisan Ales. To Øl for their simplicity, clarity, and geometricity. Prairie for their craziness and illustration style. These two breweries are polar opposites in their visual style, and that's why I admire them. ▲

VANDHGRAARS
GVMHNSXERPAS
RGHONVAE ASP
EGNARVOH SPA
GNOAEHRV PSA
NAGVERHO APS
HERANOOV SPA
RAHNGEVO PAS
ANVGHORE ASP
HANGOVER SAP

3 HOPS × 3 CITRUS IPA

Edit   +

KVEIK
Alarm

ME UP
Alarm

WHEN
Alarm

SEPTEMBER
Alarm

ENDS
Alarm

KVEIK IPA DDH CITRA + SABRO

LOCAL & CRAFT
ST. PETERSBURG
2012

BROUWERIJ
DE MOLEN

KUPOLA & PASTILA
UNORTHODOX DESSERT IMPERIAL STOUT

LERVIG

YEAR OF FEAR
CLAUSTROPHOBIC IMPERIAL STOUT
AGED IN KENTUCKY BARRELS

Oddity Brewing

LOCATION
Barcelona, Spain

DESIGN
Dani R. Feria, Alberto Miranda, Bea Salas, Txemy, Kim Van Vuuren

Spanish brewers of soft-spoken beers and dark ales, Oddity puts equal care into their highly Instagrammable labels, each created by a different artist tasked with transmitting the souls of their recipes.

Oddity
brewing

Crumbling Crowd BROWN STOUT

Crumbling Crowd BROWN STOUT

BEER, BIERE, ØL CERVEZA, BIRRA

MALT:BARLEY, OATS, BROWN AMBER ROASTED
HOPS: COLUMBUS

Es: Agua, Cebada, Avena, Lupulo Y Levadura
Cat: Aigua, Ordi, Civada, Llúpol I Llevat
En: Water, Barley, Oats, Hops And Yeast
It: Acqua, Orzo, Avena, Luppolo E Lievito
Fr: Eau, Orge, Avoine, Houblon Et Levure
Dk: Vand, Byg, Havre, Humle, Gær
Se: Vatten, Korn, Havre, Humle, Jäst

Contiene: Gluten, Cebada, Trigo, Avena
Conte: Gluten, Ordi, Civada, Blat
Contains: Gluten, Barley, Oats, Wheat
Contiene: Glutine, Orzo, Avena, Frumento
Contient: Gluten, Orge, Blé, Avoine
Inhold: Gluten, Byg, Havre, Hvede
Innehåller: Gluten, Kornmalt, Havre, Vete

Oddity Brewing
Designed in **Barcelona**
Brewed by **Oddity**
at **Whiplash Beer** Ltd
artwork by: **@txemy**
www.odditybrewing.es

5391533331552

6.0% ALC VOL
2.6 UK UNITS
440ML

STORE COLD
DON'T AGE
DRINK FRESH

How would you describe the visual style of your brewery?

Dani R. Feria (Graphic Designer): We create each label with a different artist, and that's a challenge in terms of maintaining a strong brand image. We rely on a fairly rigid grid that also allows freedom for artists to operate. Something like Swiss design partying with its wildest friends—it may seem crazy, but it all turns out surprisingly well. A mix of bold fonts, noticeable lines, vibrant colors, and somewhat trippy images open to interpretation.

Vicky Navarro (Co-Founder and Brand Manager): Collaborating with different artists was part of the idea from the start: Ivan Raho would make modern, hoppy beers, and I would try to make Oddity breathe creatively and be in constant motion. These collaborations help us keep evolving and listening to new ideas.

What is the process for designing the label for a new release?

DRF: Everything starts with giving the artist the name, variety, and characteristics. Once the artist sends us a proposal, we work together to find a color palette that adapts and gives strength to the illustration. This is often the most complex part, as it consists of balancing and giving space to both the voice of the artist and that of the brand.

Where does the inspiration for the labels come from?

DRF: Emotional states, vital moments, or comical situations are the starting point of all our creations.

VN: Finding a new name for each beer becomes a game, because there is little left to invent. Normally, Ivan and I start spouting words and concepts that make us think about that beer, what we want it to convey or the situation in which the recipe was conceived. We have the freedom to come up with anything—the difficult part comes later, which is transmitting that idea to the artist. Man Behind the Scene, for example, is a tribute to all the people behind Oddity, who make us who we are. Youngsters on Dominoes came to mind as we were watching our uncles reveal their fiery sides during a game of dominoes. There, There is inspired by a Radiohead song and came at a time when we needed to calm down, gather strength, and move forward—because Oddity was born in the middle of the pandemic.

Which of your labels are you most proud of?

DRF: Probably the most recent label because little by little we push the limits and feel more comfortable to do crazy things and have fun.

What role do your visual identity and beer labels play in the success of your brand?

DRF: We see our labels as a blank canvas that we give to the artist. We also create a very careful visual universe with photography, our website that uses typographic compositions more typical of a magazine, and even the crazy idea of printing our last line of T-shirts ourselves.

VN: I think people realize there is good teamwork behind the image of Oddity, and we try to transfer that spirit to social networks, our merch, and everything we do.

Can you name two breweries whose visual styles you admire?

DRF: Half Full, for their good aesthetic taste and their campaign to destigmatize mental-health problems, which is amazing. A little closer to home, Soma's work will always have a space in our hearts.

VN: I love everything at Grimm Artisanal Ales in Brooklyn—their logo, the fun and colorful illustrations of the labels, the photos they post on social media, and even the design of their taproom. I really like the work Sophie De Vere does at Whiplash. The labels are instantly recognizable by their white background and Sophie's collages, which are psychedelic and humorous. ▲

> # We rely on a fairly rigid grid that also allows freedom for artists to operate. Something like Swiss design partying with its wildest friends.
>
> DANI R. FERIA
> *Graphic Designer*

Rascals Brewing Company

LOCATION
Dublin, Ireland

—

DESIGN
Triona O'Donoghue

With attention-grabbing typography and vivid color palettes, Dublin's Rascals Brewing Company wants drinkers to broaden their tastes and have fun doing it.

How would you describe the visual style of your brewery?

Triona O'Donoghue (Designer): Fun, bright, eye-catching, and bursting with color and imagination. To add to our customers' experience of the beer, each can has a fun name, and we include an illustrative beer education on the back. We think of the core range as a kind of home-base, so the graphics are simple, hand-rendered typography with beer names that give a little education on the style and taste. Each core beer has a striking color to convey their uniqueness and stand apart from each other, while still ensuring the brand identity is communicated collectively. To contrast this, the specials are designed to inspire people to be a little bit adventurous. Typography is still front and center, but we use bright illustrations and patterns and often add an offbeat twist.

What is the process for designing the label for a new release?

TO: The starting point is the name. Beer names are thrown about with Rascals' marketing manager Joe Donnelly and owner Emma Devlin. Joe's voice perfectly reflects the brand's personality, and he has come up with most of the names! The beer concept and name lock in the visual direction for me. I research, then mood board and sketch a few ideas using pen and paper or Procreate. Then I will show the team, and once we are happy, I plow ahead and finalize the design.

Where does the inspiration for the labels come from?

TO: The beer concept dictates where I search for inspiration. Sometimes they have very specific threads to follow. For example, with Chai So Serious I researched exquisite ▶

Indian patterns and typography. India has a wealth of beautiful hand-drawn typography, from trucks to hotel signage, so the resources were endless. Then Betty and Bruce were very interesting beers to design, as the motivation was to celebrate and honor a culture while being culturally sensitive. The research for this was a lot more reading-based.

Which of your labels are you most proud of?

TO: My more recent 440 ml special labels because of the journey I am on with these graphically. I have felt a personal shift in trusting my ability to communicate using more illustrative and ornate typography. Since I moved over to the iPad I can lose myself in the artwork; it feels so akin to drawing on paper, which feels very natural and gives better results.

What role do your visual identity and beer labels play in the success of your brand?

TO: Of course I want the beers to be commercially successful, but another big motivation for me is to bring more beauty to a product that will exist with or without me. I want to add an extra lovely moment to a drinker's experience and hopefully, in a tiny way, enhance their enjoyment of the beer. The care, attention, and creativity you see on the can art directly reflect the care, attention, and creativity in every other area of the company, because we genuinely care how people experience the beer. I think there is an honesty in that, which separates us from others (and especially the macro-breweries) and adds to the brand's success.

Can you name two breweries whose visual styles you admire?

TO: I admire the quietness of Cloudwater's visual style. They use surreal collages depicting natural beauty spots, and the visuals are so beautiful to look at while you are having a can of their beer. I think it adds some lovely downtime to the beer experience. I have always liked Brixton Brewery with their strong typographic B supported by funky, beautiful patterns. I am also a sucker for a nice print finish or spot gloss. ▲

> ## Typography is still front and center, but we use bright illustrations and patterns and often add an offbeat twist.
>
> TRIONA O'DONOGHUE
> *Designer*

Stigbergets

LOCATION
Gothenburg, Sweden

DESIGN
Neale Payling

The award-winning Swedish makers of hazy, hoppy beers, Stigbergets features a hand-drawn menagerie of creatures on their distinctive, off-beat cans.

How would you describe the visual style of your brewery?

Neale Payling (Designer): Bold, colorful, and often with just a single element in focus—usually an animal or weird creature of some kind. I paint everything by hand including most typography, which I think gives the labels a nice warm and cozy feeling.

What is the process for designing the label for a new release?

NP: The brewery comes to me with a name (and sometimes an animal in mind), and then I'll start sketching. If the brewery likes it, I get straight to painting the thing. After that it's a laborious process of scanning stuff in and piecing it together on the computer. We also have a few more "templated" designs with a more graphic style, like the recent Ringöbräu series, which is also hand drawn but much easier to make variations of with different colors.

Where does the inspiration for the labels come from?

NP: The people at the brewery come up with all the beer names, which are often inspired by music in one way or another, be it lyrics or old song titles. My inspiration for the painting style often comes from old vintage posters and nature illustrations.

Which of your labels are you most proud of?

NP: Well, it's not a label at all but closely tied to the brewery—the book *Boken om öl och andra goda grejer (The Book About Beer and Other Tasty Things)* which is a beer/food recipe book written by the brewery together with a chef. It has a bunch of different illustrations from labels over the years, as well as new ones.

What role do your visual identity and beer labels play in the success of your brand?

NP: I try not to get too caught up in what sells the most. Sometimes I'll hear that a label I was proud of maybe wasn't a best seller, or that one I'm less proud of was a hit. But overall I think that Stigbergets has developed a distinctive style that a lot of people appreciate and enjoy, so I've no doubt that it plays a role. The beer does taste nice, which might also help.

Can you name two breweries whose visual styles you admire?

NP: I'm a big fan of Prairie Artisan Ales, even though I've never tasted or even seen one of their beers in real life. I love the humor in the ideas and the style they are drawn in. Then there's Partizan Brewing from the U.K.—I have been a huge fan of Alec Doherty's illustrations for ages. I even bought one of his rings for my wedding ring! I like the way he creates such complete illustrations with such simple lines and shapes. ▲

> **My inspiration for the painting style often comes from old vintage posters and nature illustrations.**
>
> NEALE PAYLING
> *Designer*

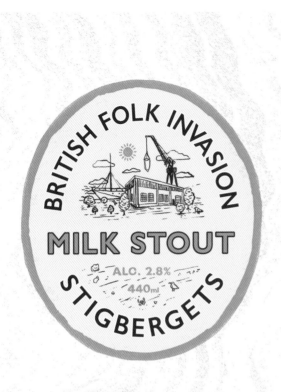

Omnipollo

LOCATION
Stockholm, Sweden

———

DESIGN
Karl Grandin

An innovative partnership between a brewer and a graphic artist,
Omnipollo has a synergy between beer and design that has
produced some of the scene's most artful and arresting labels.

How would you describe the visual style of your brewery?

Karl Grandin (Artist and Co-Founder): Unconsciously suggestive.

What is the process for designing the label for a new release?

KG: Instead of making artwork that is meant to describe or portray the style or taste of a beer, I try to capture something else and focus on the vibe and the ideas surrounding the product. Some need more preparation or interaction before the pen hits paper, but once I've started I go about it more or less the same way—trying to pour my mind into images, guided by memories and thoughts recorded in my sketchbooks. Every Omnipollo design has an individual concept and narrative, but together they build on a greater story, a world that keeps changing, expanding, and evolving.

Where does the inspiration for the labels come from?

KG: The unconscious, dreams, daydreams, and the people around me. Sometimes I need to lock myself in my studio to work in seclusion, but I usually can't stay away from the outside world for too many days. It's important for me to be with creatures that inspire me, and that's the main reason I work on collaborative projects, such as Omnipollo, rather than just drawing and painting for myself only.

Which of your labels are you most proud of?

KG: I enjoy them all for different reasons. I like the Leon and Mazarin bottles because they set the tone for what we have been doing visually and conceptually, and Light Light Light because it felt like a new direction for us at the time. I'm also happy with the latest version of Gone that was released in January 2021. Hopefully the next label will be the one I'm most excited about. ▶

What role do your visual identity and beer labels play in the success of your brand?

KG: There is always a synergy between the concoction, the artwork, and the title of the Omnipollo products, sometimes straightforward and sometimes more cryptic. It is hard to tell what part the imagery has played in the impact of the brand, but I hope the artwork has opened a few eyes and hopefully some minds along the way.

Can you name two breweries whose visual styles you admire?

KG: Two artists whose beer-related work I like are Tiago Majuelos and Keith Shore, for Birrificio La Gramigna and Mikkeller, respectively. I like brands that dare to do their own thing. There is no set formula, we should make the rules up as we go along. ▲

Every Omnipollo design has an individual concept and narrative, but together they build on a greater story, a world that keeps changing, expanding, and evolving.

KARL GRANDIN
Artist and Co-Founder

Balter

LOCATION
Currumbin,
Australia

———

DESIGN
Balter and
Lachie Goldsworthy

The smile on every can of Balter sums up the Gold Coast-brewery's mission: to spread joy with good beer.

How would you describe the visual style of your brewery?

Stirling Howland (Co-Founder and Brand Director): Minimal. This is probably an understatement but our whole premise when setting up Balter was, let's not design just for design's sake. We are very much about form and function, and we love design that can achieve both.

What is the process for designing the label for a new release?

SH: Coming up with a beer is the first part, then a name. Both these things dictate the design of the can. From there it's just picking it apart until we are happy with it.

Where does the inspiration for the labels come from?

SH: We wanted our branding to be approach-able and easy to understand but to function and stand out in any environment. We all know craft-beer fridges, bottle shops, and bars are very busy spaces. So when we were looking at standing out in these environments, we were kind of happy when we realized that minimal was going to get it done. In terms of more bespoke can labels, the name usually poses an inspiration—for example, Handsome Elvis has jailhouse stripes. You notice no Balter branding on the front, just a reliance on the rectangle and smile.

Which of your labels are you most proud of?

SH: Probably our XPA can. This was our first beer launched to market and has taken Australia by storm. When we launched there wasn't anything like this in beer from a design sense, color palette, or flavor, so to see it connect the way it has is a really nice feeling.

What role do your visual identity and beer labels play in the success of your brand?

SH: Our XPA can, with its seafoam green color and smile is the most iconic part of our brand identity. Everything we do in marketing features these elements and it's definitely worked for us in terms of building a recognizable brand no matter where it's sitting. This formula has then been translated into the other beers we have launched. Our smile is also a symbol of enjoyment— everything we love about beer. As a brand, we've always demonstrated that what happens around beer is equal to the beer itself, and that smile influences every facet of our company from our culture to what we create to the way we communicate. We have found people are drawn to that smile for so many reasons.

Can you name two breweries whose visual styles you admire?

SH: I'd say Garage Project. They are the antithesis of us from a design sense, but their art is a natural extension of who they are as people. And another Kiwi brewery, Parrotdog—I love their logo and how it boldly fits anywhere. They have wonderful copy, and they're epic people as well. ▲

We wanted our branding to be approachable and easy to understand but to function and stand out in any environment.

STIRLING HOWLAND
Co-Founder and Brand Director

FELL ON DANK DAYS
WEST COAST IPA

BALTER & FIRESTONE WALKER

BALTER

With enjoyment.

LIMITED
RELEASE

THE GODFATHER
IIPA

BALTER & STONE BREWING

BALTER

With enjoyment.

LIMITED
RELEASE

MOXEE SUNSET
PNW PALE ALE

BALTER & BALEBREAKER

BALTER

With enjoyment.

LIMITED
RELEASE

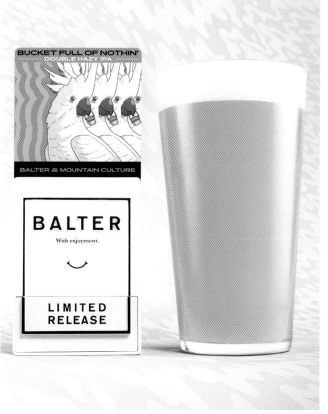

BUCKET FULL OF NOTHIN'
DOUBLE HAZY IIPA

BALTER & MOUNTAIN CULTURE

BALTER

With enjoyment.

LIMITED
RELEASE

HANDSOME

ELVIS

375ML

Polly's Brew Co.

LOCATION
Mold, U.K.

DESIGN
Sean Wheldon

Polly's
Double India Pale Ale
'Nada'

A close-knit team operating from a farm in small-town Wales, Polly's Brew Co. stands out with audacious label designs and a dedication to brewing up fresh, modern, hop-forward styles.

How would you describe the visual style of your brewery?

Arron Fellows (Head of Sales): Our visual style is centered around bold, eye-catching label designs that maintain an element of simplicity at the same time. All our beers follow the same basic structure: our droplet logo as the centerpiece, with an interchangeable photo background.

What is the process for designing the label for a new release?

AF: It's not a massively complex process; we have our basic template, which was designed two years ago, and our owner Sean scours his way through stock photography and finds a part of the photograph that works well with both the theme of the beer and his ethos of boldness and simplicity.

Where does the inspiration for the labels come from?

AF: I think some inspiration has come from the early Cloudwater labels, which had plain white labels with interchangeable artwork from local artists. Our vision for our labels has been very clear from day one though—basic layout of the can labels with a rotating stock photo as the background.

Which of your labels are you most proud of?

AF: There are a few that are my personal favorites: Patternist, Nada, and Every Piece Matters immediately come to mind, but I'm proud of pretty much all of them—they're as much a part of the brewery as the liquid inside the cans.

What role do your visual identity and beer labels play in the success of your brand?

AF: I think without the visual identity of the can labels, we may not be where we are today. Even on our first releases, the feedback was highly praising of the artwork we'd used. I think the Instagrammability of the can labels is something Sean was very conscious of, and people sharing photos of these beers on their social media channels has been integral.

Can you name two breweries whose visual styles you admire?

AF: Cloudwater is certainly one we've drawn a lot of inspiration from. I'm also a big fan of the way North Brewing Co. is able to utilize simple abstract vector artwork and create something new and visually appealing each time. ▲

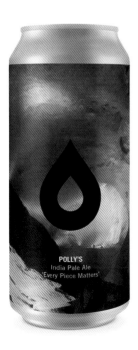

Index

Craft Beer Design

The Design, Illustration, and Branding of Contemporary Breweries

This book was conceived by *Peter Monrad*.
Edited and designed by *gestalten*.

Edited by *Robert Klanten*
Co-edited by *Peter Monrad*

Text and introduction by *Peter Monrad*

Editorial Management by *Sam Stevenson*

Design by *Isabelle Emmerich*

Layout by *Isabelle Emmerich* and *Melanie Ullrich*

Cover by *Melanie Ullrich*

Typefaces: Acumin by *Robert Slimbach*
and Plantin by *Monotype*

Cover images by Mikkeller (top);
Celestial Beerworks, photo: Sara Morton
(center left); Halo Brewery, photo: Daniel
Ehrenworth (center right); Archetype Brewing
(bottom left); Fuerst Wiacek, photo: Domagoj
Kunić (bottom right)
Backcover images by Japas Cervejaria, photo:
Gothard (top left); Beak Brewery, photo: Sam
A Harris (top right); Play Brew Co. (bottom)

Printed by
Schleunungdruck GmbH, Marktheidenfeld
Made in Germany

Published by gestalten, Berlin 2022
ISBN 978-3-96704-032-6

For more information, and to order books, please visit
www.gestalten.com

Bibliographic information published by the Deutsche
Nationalbibliothek. The Deutsche Nationalbibliothek
lists this publication in the Deutsche National-
bibliografie; detailed bibliographic data is available
online at www.dnb.de

None of the content in this book was published in
exchange for payment by commercial parties or
designers; the inclusion of all work is based solely
on its artistic merit.